# SWEDENBORG

## AND THE SAPIENTA ANGELICA

First Edition 1910
Frank Sewall

New Edition 2020
Edited by Tarl Warwick

# COPYRIGHT AND DISCLAIMER

# FOREWORD

This work here is a compilation, in essence, one part autobiography of Swedenborg, one part semi-exhaustive list of his works then available (both in English and other languages, on various topics), and partially a largely accepting discussion of his beliefs.

The man himself- Swedenborg- is an interesting character about which debate even exists today; some chalk his visions and spiritual encounters (through which, he claims, he spoke directly with angels and was given divine revelations) up to madness, others to being nothing but the writings of an opportunistic charlatan. Others follow his teachings more or less literally, and there are those today who consider him to be a sort of prophet. Regardless, we know he was a true Renaissance Man, developing various scientific theories especially on the subject of anatomy that predate their acceptance by a very long period; indeed, he arguably invented the basic concept of neurons long before mankind was capable of seeing their form.

The autobiographical material here is broken into stages according to the things he was doing in those times and lists various works and their basic content as well which he made; mostly spiritual but in the first eras of his life, mostly technological and academic.

This edition of "Swedenborg and the Sapienta Angelica" has been carefully edited for format and content. Care has been taken to retain all original intent and meaning.

# SWEDENBORG AND THE SAPIENTA ANGELICA

## CHAPTER I: YOUTH AND EARLY STUDIES

Of Dalecarlian ancestry, his grandfathers on both sides being peasant mine-owners in Fahlun, Sweden, Emanuel Swedenborg was born in Stockholm on the twenty-ninth day of January, 1688. He was the second son of Jesper Swedberg, at that time an army chaplain, but later made Dean and Professor of Theology at Upsala, and thence promoted to be the Bishop of Skara in West Gothland, his episcopal charge embracing also the Swedish settlements in America.

The family name was Isaacson, the name Swedberg being derived from "Sweden," the name of their mining property in Fahlun, the title Swedenborg being conferred with the rank of nobility given to the family by Queen Ulrica Eleanor in 1719, when Emanuel took his seat in the House of Nobles.

Entering the University of Upsala in 1699 at the early age of eleven years, he pursued his studies in the faculty of philosophy until his twenty-first year, in 1709. His brother-in-law, Eric Benzelius, the university librarian, a learned scholar, afterwards appointed archbishop, encouraged the young student's zeal for mathematics and the physical sciences, and offered to supplement the somewhat reluctant and chary provision of his father for further study by aiding him to make a tour abroad. He was eager to be released from study and paternal control, and to gain touch with the real world, which seemed impossible under the limited resources and the cramped scholasticism of the university, where the lively controversy was still waging by the Cartesians for the introduction of modern methods. His bent for the classics and his youthful love of verse are shown in his graduation thesis on the Morals of Seneca, and a number of festive odes and other poems in Latin, some of which were published later under the title of Ludus Heliconicus and Carmena Borea. But his real aim was for a deeper and wider knowledge of nature.

In the year 1710, with his brother-in-law's assistance, he went abroad for a tour of five years, embracing England, Holland, France and Germany. He spent a year in London and Oxford, making the acquaintance of Flamsteed and Halley, and, as he reports to his brother-in-law, "studying Newton daily," with the result that he became more and more impatient of the slow progress of his native country in the mathematical and physical sciences. As for himself he would "invent something new every day"; and he urgently recommends the Upsala University to obtain a better salary for the mathematical professor by cutting down, if necessary, appropriations for the theological and historical faculties. To make himself master of mechanical appliances he took up his lodgings successively with a watchmaker, a cabinet-maker, an instrument-maker and a grinder of lenses; and a list of his own projected inventions at this time includes a flying machine, a submarine war-vessel, a quick-firing gun, an air-pump and a mechanical piano player. Returning to Sweden in 1715, he begins, under the patronage of the young King Charles XII., the publication, in the following year, of a mathematical journal, the Daedalus Hyperboreum; and in 1718 he published an Algebra in ten books, it being the first work on that branch of mathematics published in the Swedish language; and so backward were his countrymen in this branch of science that "he feared he would find no one capable of correcting the printer's proofs."

Before leaving home he had enjoyed the acquaintance and friendship of the distinguished engineer Polhem; and on his return, King Charles XII., struck by the genius and ability of the young inventor, called him to the service of the Government as an assistant to Polhem and as an extraordinary Assessor in the

College of Mines. Two years later, during the attack on the Norwegian fortress of Frederickshall, where the king met his death, Swedenborg planned the successful transportation of the king's galleys overland for seventeen miles from Stromstad to Iddefjord. His published treatises on mathematics and the industrial arts at this time include such subjects as the *Manufacture of Tin Plate and its Use*, the *Level of the Sea and the Tides of the Ancient World* and *Information about Docks, Sluices and Salt Works*. While associated with Polhem in his engineering undertakings and a frequent and welcome visitor at his house, Swedenborg fell in love with one of Polhem's daughters; but notwithstanding the favor with which the match was regarded by both the father and the king, his offer of marriage was rejected and Swedenborg remained unmarried. His position as Assessor at the Royal College of Mines he held until the year 1747, when, at his own request, he was retired on a pension of half his salary.

## CHAPTER II: COSMOGONY AND PHYSICS

### 1721-1734

In 1721 Swedenborg commenced his second tour on the Continent, and published in Amsterdam his Studies in Chemistry, a Prodromus, or forecast of his Principia, wherein he attempts to reduce the phenomena of nature to a geometrical system. He published his *Observations and Discoveries respecting Iron and Fire; A New Method of finding Longitudes by Lunar Observations* and other works pertaining to mechanics. In Leipzig appeared, in 1772, his *Miscellaneous Observations connected with the Physical Sciences*, and twelve years later, also at Leipzig, under the munificent patronage of Ludwig Rudolph, Duke of Brunswick, the stately folios of the *Opera Philosophica et Mineralia*, containing, for their first part, the *Principia Rerum Naturalium*, or *New Attempts toward the Philosophical Explanation of the Elementary World.*

The Principia, after an introductory chapter on "The Means Conducive to a True Philosophy," presents in Part I. "A Philosophical Argument concerning the 'First Simple'" from which the world with its natural things originated; that is, concerning the First Natural Point and its Existence from the Infinite. Thus he begins his argument:

"There is a first entity produced from the Infinite, for the finite cannot exist per se, therefore it must exist by means of that which can produce what is finite, and which is infinite per se. Therefore, composite things derive their origin from simples from the Infinite, and the Infinite from itself, which is also the cause of itself and of all things. The simple is the first entity existing by motion from the Infinite, and thus in regard to existence it is a medium between the Infinite and the finite. For it is by the mediation of this point, or most simple entity, that finite things exist from the Infinite. This point is immediately produced from the Infinite, and its origin is purely a motion in the universal Infinite which is pure and total motion, and cannot be conceived of geometrically." Later, he defines this origin of the point, and so of the created universe, as a "conatus of motion in the Infinite."... "In this (effort towards motion) lies concentrated all that quality which, is capable of bringing into act finite things, together with all their modes and contingencies, and even of producing the world itself." (*Principia*, 22).

The argument discusses the First Finite and its origin from Points; the Second Finite and its origin from the Simple Finite, and so on to the Active of the First Finite, its motion, figure, state, etc., showing that this Active is one with and constitutes the sun of our system, and that in like manner it forms the first elementary particles. Further on are described the First and most Universal Element; the Actives of the Second and Third Finite; the Third Finite, or Substantial; the Magnetic, or Second Element of the World, its motion, figure, attributes and modes; and finally the existence of the Sun and the formation of the Solar Vortex. Part II. treats of the Causes and Mechanism of the Magnetic Forces: the influence of the Magnet upon Iron, the Disjunctive and Repulsive Forces etc., etc., and the Declination of the Magnet. Part III. treats of the Starry Heaven as compared with the Magnetic Sphere, of the Diversity of Worlds, of the Fourth Finite, the Universal Solar and Planetary Chaos, and its separation into Planets and Satellites, the Ether, or Third Element of the World, the Fifth Finite, the Air, or Fourth Element of our System, of Fire, of Water, of the Purely Material Finite, of Vapor, of the Vortex surrounding the Earth, of the Paradise formed upon our Earth, and of the First Man. This vast work of the Principia marks the advance of Swedenborg's mind from the scientific to the philosophic plane; it deals with what is imponderable and invisible, and what can only be apprehended by the imagination; and yet the whole realm of elementary being, thus regarded, is treated with rigid geometrical and mathematical precision and logic. Swedenborg calls his work "philosophical"; but by philosophy he here means "the knowledge of the mechanism of our world, or of whatever in the world is subject to the laws of geometry, or which it is possible to unfold to view by experience assisted by geometry and reason." (Principia, ch. i). The successive steps in the evolution, through the procession of Simples, Finites and Actives, of a visible universe, follow in rational order from the assumed vortical motion of the First Simple to the stability and order of our solar system, the relation and movement of star-groups and an explanation of the Milky Way.

As in the *Chemistry* (1721) we find a science of the invisibles such as Tyndall has later contended for, treating of bodies in their elementary forms and relations, so in the Principia is given a complete theory of Evolution, embracing Motions and Forms, the nature and functions of the successive Auras, the laws of Vibratory Currents and the Magnetic Force. The importance of Swedenborg's contributions to physical science, not only in theories anticipating modern discoveries, but in principles of permanent value in the pursuance of research, is beginning to receive extraordinary acknowledgment. Of the doctrines of the first forms of matter, in the early work on Chemistry, published in 1721, Van't Hoff, in his introduction to the *Arrangement of Atoms in Space*, translated by Eiloart, says that they embody the germs of the modern science of Crystallography or Stereo-Chemistry. Of Swedenborg's early geological treatises, Professor A. C. Nathorst, of the Royal Swedish Academy, says:

"Swedenborg's contributions in the field of geology are of such importance and scope that alone they would have been sufficient to have secured him a respected scientific name: still, these works are but the minor portion of his whole scientific activity, which in many respects was far ahead of the times. For he was also a mathematician, astronomer, cosmologist, physicist, mechanic, chemist, anatomist, and physiologist. What Anders

Retzius said concerning the Regnum Animale, that it was a 'wonder-book' in which are found 'ideas belonging to the most recent times, a compass, induction and tendency which can only be compared to that of Aristotle,' seems, after the experience now attained, to be capable of application to the whole of his scientific activity (Introduction to the Geologica et Epistolce). In the Royal Swedish Academy's edition of Swedenborg's Scientific Works, containing his contributions to cosmology, Svante Arrhenius makes the following recognition:

'If we briefly summarize the ideas which were first given expression to by Swedenborg and afterwards, although usually in a much mollified form, consciously or unconsciously taken up by other authors in cosmology, we find them to be the following. 'The planets of our solar system originate from the solar matter: taken up by Buffon, Kant, Laplace and others. The earth and the other planets have gradually removed themselves from the sun, and received a gradually lengthened time of revolution; a view expressed by G. H. Darwin. The earth's time of rotation, that is to say, the day's length, has been greatly increased; a view again expressed by G. H. Darwin. The suns are arranged around a milky way; taken up by Wright, Kant and Lambert. There are still greater systems in which the milky ways are arranged; taken up by Lambert.' (Introduction to the *Cosmologia*; vol. ii. Of edition mentioned above)."

"It cannot be disputed that the real germ of the nebular hypothesis, namely, the idea that the entire solar system has formed itself out of a single chaotic mass which rolled itself at first into a colossal sphere, and afterwards threw off a ring, which through continuous rotation at length broke into parts, these finally contracting into balls, planets that this idea first found utterance in Swedenborg. Kant's work on the same subject appeared twenty-one years later, and Laplace published his hypothesis sixty-two years later." See Article in *Vierteljahrschrift der Astronomischen Gesellschaft* p. 8: Leipzig,

# SWEDENBORG

1879; *Swedenborg and the Nebular Hypothesis* by Magnus Nyren, Ph.D., Astronomer at the Observatory at Pulkowa, Russia.

## CHAPTER III: PHYSIOLOGY AND PSYCHOLOGY

### 1734-1745

From the survey of the universe as a macrocosm, subject to the laws of mechanics and geometry, the author's studies now reach forth to the Nature of the Infinite, its connection with the finite, and the soul of man. He publishes, in Dresden and Leipzig, in 1734, a *Prodromus de Infinite et Causa Finali Creationis* ("Outlines on the Infinite and the Final Cause of Creation, and on the Mechanism of the Intercourse between the Soul and the Body"). Here he carries his mechanical and geometric method over into the most subtle realm of research, producing the outlines of a physiological psychology which may seem at first to assert an almost ultra-materialistic view; yet he says to those who complain of his reduction of all things to mechanical law, "It matters not if it be called a mechanism, provided it is always an animated mechanism." For this term, "an animated mechanism" truly characterizes his entire view of the world; a system shaped and dominated by a Power and an *anima* above nature as a body by its soul.

Of the seven years of travel which now followed in Germany, France and Italy he has left an interesting journal in his *Itineraria*, showing the wide range of his observations and interest, from the working of salt-mines and blasting furnaces, the discipline of troops, the merits of the various political constitutions of countries visited, to the aesthetics and ethics of religious ceremonials, the attractions of the opera and the beauty of public buildings and works of art. What may be termed his philosophical period closed with the production in London, 1740-45, of the two great works The Economy of the Animal Kingdom, considered Anatomically, Physically, and Philosophically (*Economia Regni Animalis*), and the Animal Kingdom (*Regnum Animale*).

In these works he confesses that his search is for nothing less than the soul itself. The search follows, indeed, in orderly sequence, as outlined in the Introduction to the Principia, where he says: "Under the empire of geometry, and under the mechanical laws of motion, we place the whole mineral, as well as the whole vegetable kingdom, and indeed the animal, too, with respect to mechanical organs, muscles, fibers, and membranes, or with respect to its anatomical, vegetative and organic relations; but with respect to the soul and its various faculties I do not think it possible that they can be explained or comprehended by any laws of motion known to us. Though the world is mechanical, and composed of a series of finite things which originate by means of the most varied contingents, and, being such, may be explored by means of experiment and phenomena, it does not follow that all things in the world are subject to the laws of geometry.

For there are innumerable things that are not mechanical or even geometrical, such as the Infinite and whatever is in the Infinite. We may learn the mechanism of the organs of the body, how they are moved by muscles, tendons, fibers, and nerves; how the undulating air is received by the membranes of the ear, and is represented in the chamber of the brain by means of sound; how the ether exhibits a modification of itself in the eye, and runs through the tissues of the nerves till it meets the meninges of the brain... We see every emotion and mode of the soul exhibited mechanically in the body. But, after all, what that intelligence is in the soul which knows, and is able to determine, to choose, to let one thing pass out into act and not another, of this we are obviously ignorant." (Principia, ch. i.).

The knowledge of the soul is now to be his quest. The Regnum Animale means to him the soul's domain, the human body. Here he will learn what the soul is, and the modes of its abode in and control over, not the body alone, but over all the forces of nature; since "in man the world is concentrated, and in him, as in a microcosm, the whole universe may be contemplated from the beginning to the end."

Of these two works, the Economia and the Regnum Animale, only a portion was published by the author. Of the unpublished portions, the treatise on The Brain (*De Cerebro*) has been in part translated from the photo-lithographed MSS., and published in London: James Spiers, 1882. The complete work on The Soul, or Rational Psychology (*De Anima*, etc.), has been translated from the posthumous Latin edition and published in New York, 1886.

The author's desire to be guided by the simple facts of nature unbiased by prejudice, or by the ambition to establish a theory, is shown by his unwillingness to rely upon his own experiments, and his availing himself of the highest scientific authorities extant. It is only fair, therefore, that the defects that have been pointed out in some of his scientific data should be attributed to the crudeness of scientific knowledge in his day, rather than to the general principles he was endeavoring to illustrate. Of Swedenborg's anatomical and physiological discoveries, the distinguished anatomist, Dr. Gustav Retzius thus gives his judgment in his address at Heidelberg, in 1903, before the Congress of Anatomists, over which body he was presiding.

"Emanuel Swedenborg was not only a great expert in the knowledge of the brain according to the standard of his time, but in fundamental questions he was far in advance of his contemporaries. If we ask for the reason, we can only find it in the fact that Swedenborg was not only a learned anatomist and skilled observer, but that he was a deep and critical anatomical thinker. He stands out in the history of craniology as a single, wonderful, phenomenal spirit and ideal seeker of the truth, who, step by step, grasped at ever higher problems. One can understand more easily his life and his work when one combines his achievements in anatomy and physiology with those in geology, mechanics, cosmogony, and physics. With this as a background, his whole aim becomes more manifest. He sought in all to find the principle of the unity of the world and of life. He believed that this fundamental principle was to be found in motion, in the tremulation of the finest particles. It was this principle that led him ever farther on into an almost universal research, and to an insight into the nature and workings of creation that was truly wonderful in his time. Led on by this controlling view (of vibratory motion) he arrived at knowledges and constructed theories which only at the present day are beginning to receive an appreciative recognition."

The special localization of intellectual functions in the brain, the coincident respiration of brain and lungs, the vitality of the blood, and the process by which sensation becomes converted into imagination and idea by a series and correspondence of the subtle tremulations in the respective substances in which they occur, are among the subjects treated with great clearness and lucidity in these remarkable volumes. The Animal Kingdom, than which title that of the Soul-Kingdom would more accurately convey the meaning of the original Regnum Animale, included a great series, parts of which were not published until after the author's death, including two of the volumes on the Brain, the volume on Generation, the Soul, or Rational Psychology, and special treatises on the Senses, the Fiber, etc.

The volumes published by Swedenborg treat of the following subjects. In the Economy of the Animal Kingdom: The Composition and General Essence of the Blood, its Circulation, the Formation of the Chick in the Egg, the Circulation of the Blood in the Fetus, the Motion of the Adult Heart, the Motion of the Brain, its Animation coincident with the Respiration of the Lungs, the Cortical Substance of the Brain, and the Human Soul. In the Animal Kingdom: The Tongue, Lips, Mouth, etc., the Stomach and other Intestines; the Nose, Larynx, etc.; the Lungs and Pleura; the Diaphragm; the Skin and Sense of Touch, the Use of Touch and the Sense of Taste.

In all these researches the author was content with nothing short of a definite knowledge of the soul itself. "Bending my course inward continually, I shall open all doors that lead to her" he says, "and by Divine permission contemplate the soul herself." In the work on The Soul we find a symmetrical and exhaustive treatise on Physiological Psychology ranging in its discussions from the Simple Fiber, the proper animal essence that "Form of Forms, celestial and immortal by nature," to the Senses, the Intellect, the Mind in its three planes as Animus, Mens, and Anima, and the Affections proper to each; the Pure Intellect; and the Soul in its Immortal State; concluding with a sublime sociological forecast or conception of a Society of immortal souls as the end of creation and the realization of the City of God.

"The end of creation, or the end on account of which the world was created, could be no other than the first and the last, or the most universal of all ends, and that which is perpetually reigning in the created universe, which is the complex of means conspiring to that end. No other end of creation can be given than that there may exist a universal society of souls, or a heaven; that is, the kingdom of God. That this was the end of creation may be proved by innumerable arguments. For it would be absurd to say that the world was created on account of the earth and terrestrial societies, and this miserable and perishable life; since all things on earth are for the sake of man, and all things in man for the sake of his soul; and the soul cannot be for no end. If, then, it exists for any end, it must be for a society in which God is present; for His providence regards souls, which are spiritual, and His works are adapted to men and to their consociation."

"In order that a celestial society, or a society of souls,

may exist, it is necessary that there be a most perfect form of government, namely, souls distinct among themselves, and every possible variety, which may be called harmonies, between the souls; and so from such harmony there will arise a consensus and accord which shall produce that entire effect and end which is always foreseen and provided. That this end may be attained it is necessary that man shall be allowed a free will. The cause of variety of subjects arises solely from free exercise and liberty of the will. Without this there would be no intellect, no morality, no virtue, no vice, no crime, no guilt, no affection of the mind or change of state. This is the reason why God has wished to preserve the free human will strong and inviolate, even for the doing of evil deeds; so that we would seem to be almost willing to deny a divine Providence for the same reason that we would affirm it."

It is at the close of this work that Swedenborg presents his forecast of the *Universal Mathesis*, or a Mathematical Philosophy of Universals, which, based upon inductive knowledge of the soul's reign in the body and of certain *a priori* principles governing all of the mind's operations, extends itself into a realm of pure truth beyond science.

"There is a Science of sciences, or a universal science which contains all others in itself, and parts of which can, as it were, be resolved into these and those particular sciences. Such a science is not acquired by learning, but it is connate, especially in souls, which are pure intelligences. The soul from this science contemplates all things immediately as they are in themselves, thus whether good or evil, and according to their nature it asserts or is averse. Unless the soul were furnished with such a science it would naturally be unable to flow into our thoughts and to infuse, as it were, the power of understanding or of expressing higher things; as also it would be unable to adapt all its organic forms to the inmost and secret laws of mechanics, physics, chemistry and many other phenomena: therefore that such a science exists there can be no doubt. For there are truths *a priori*, or propositions which are at once acknowledged as true; nor is there any need of demonstration of them *a posteriori*, nor of confirmation of them from experience or by the senses. The truth itself presents itself naked, and as it were declares itself true."

"The mind is often indignant that such truths should have to be proved when they are above all demonstration. For all harmonies and thus all order naturally soothe and delight the organs of our senses, while disharmony constrains and wounds them. So it is with truths in which there is, as it were, an intellectual order. Wherefore if we were not overburdened with the fetters of science, with the turbulent desires of the lower mind and similar hindrances, we should be able to know truths purely; since a certain consent shines forth as something harmonious and as from a sacred shrine, I know not where."

In these glimpses at the possible range of knowledge of a pure soul "not overburdened with the fetters of science," we seem to have a foregleam of that higher system upon which he was entering, when, through the gate of that extraordinary experience which he describes as his illumination or intromission into the spiritual world, he is admitted into the conscious and simultaneous experience of the two worlds of man's life, and into the *sapientia angelica*. For we see here not only how the visible universe is regarded as itself an extension of the body or regnum of each soul, and the tremulations proceeding from the sun being by a continuous series of media and forms conveyed to the senses and so subjected to the soul's control, but beyond the physical world there lies yet the "shrine, I know not where," of higher essences and higher knowledges, which yet must have a place in a science which is truly perfect and universal. Throughout the whole philosophic period the devout and worshiping spirit of a seeker after not only the soul but God, its Author, is everywhere manifest. "No man" he writes, "can be a complete and truly learned philosopher without the utmost devotion to the Supreme Being. True philosophy and contempt of God are two opposites." The conception of man in his state of integrity as the true philosopher, portrayed in the Introduction to the Principia, will hardly find a rival in literature for greatness of theme couched in sublime simplicity of language.

"When the most subtle active principle of man, by the providence of God, clothed itself with a body, and added, by degrees, parts upon parts, all the motions in the most subtle elements which were present would necessarily move or affect that extremely yielding and tender substance, and would gradually impress themselves and their own mechanism upon it... The man thus formed, in whom all the parts were coordinated to receive the motions of all the elements, and to convey them successfully when received through a contiguous medium to the extremely subtle active principle, must be deemed the most perfect and the first of all men, being one in whom the connection of ends and means was continuous. So perfect a material and active being would by the senses alone in a short time become possessed of all the philosophy and experimental science natural to him; for whatever could present itself to his senses would immediately flow, by connection and contiguity, to his extremely subtle and active first principle..."

"...I have said that, in his state of integrity, man was master of a philosophy, or worldly knowledge, and this too of himself, by virtue of the perfect mechanism of his organization, that is, by nature; and thus being furnished with such excellent senses, nothing could be concealed from him, because he was formed according to all the motions and operations of the world and nature. I have said further, that nothing could exist in the world, from the regular connection of causes, which would not instantly flow, as through a most clear and pellucid medium, with a certain sensation, to the mind; that is, that all the sensations of each of his organs would penetrate to their most subtle principle, without delay, confusion, or obscurity. But when every modification in the world, of whatsoever kind, had thus arrived at its ultimate, or at his soul, it necessarily follows that his knowledge and attainments would stop there, and that he would regard and venerate, with a most profound admiration, those other and infinite things that exceeded the bounds of his intelligence; that is to say, that most vast Infinite infinitely intelligent, infinitely provident, which begins where man and his finite faculties, intelligence and providence terminate; he would see that in this Infinite all things have their being, and that from it all things have their existence..."

"...We may therefore conclude, again, that the wiser a man is, the greater are his veneration for and love of the Deity. His delights wholly terminate in the love of God a love which exhausts and replenishes all sense of delight. All the delights of the world, resulting from its variety, are nothing unless the mind also partakes of them; for no human delights can be real without the participation of the soul, since the more refined delights are lacking; and the delights which the body and soul are capable of enjoying together are not genuine and true unless they have some further connection, and terminate in the veneration and love of God; that is, unless they have reference to this love and ultimate end, in a connection with which the sense of delight most essentially consists."

It would be a grave misconception, but one into which it would be easy to fall, at this stage, to identify this knowledge declared by Swedenborg as that to be enjoyed by "those souls which are pure intelligences" with the immediate knowledge of the Gnostics, or of the various schools of theosophy and occultism which prevail in the world today. It is not the exceptional individual in this world who is to enjoy this supreme vision by means of some process of self-discipline or self-abnegation: it is rather the soul-principle in every individual that at all times possesses the universal knowledge, as that of a queen in her realm, and that makes the mind and the senses in their respective lower planes to acquire a knowledge of both the macrocosm and the microcosm of the universe at large and of the smaller but equally perfect universe of its own body. This knowledge even includes many things that never come to the individual's conscious intelligence, but remain in the secret and sacred sanctuary of the subconscious, where only the universal control of a divine guardian is active.

From the mysticism, both of the Gnostics of past ages and of the Orientalists of today, Swedenborg must be entirely sundered, for it is from an utterly different source, and by another experience altogether, and one quite unforeseen by himself, that he is to learn the true nature of the soul and of her superior knowledge.

## CHAPTER IV: THE TRANSITION

### 1745-1772

Had Swedenborg's labors ceased at this point, the knowledge of the soul would have remained where his illustrious predecessors in these investigations, from Plato down, had left it, and where Kant, his contemporary, acknowledged it must ever be left, so far as the power of pure reason is concerned a sublime speculation without the elements of certainty and reality. Swedenborg's discussion of the nature of the Pure Intellect would have, side by side with Kant's Critique of Pure Reason, challenged in friendly rivalry the admiration of the world, and the resemblance which Kant admits that he found between many of his principles and those of Swedenborg would have resulted possibly in the public's acceptance of Swedenborg's as the safer, because more logical, guide in these transcendental paths. ("The system of Swedenborg is, unfortunately, very similar to my own philosophy. It is not impossible that my rational views may be considered absurd because of that affinity. As to the offensive comparison, I declare we must either suppose greater intelligence and truth at the basis of Swedenborg's writings than first impressions excite, or that it is a mere accident when he coincides with my system." (*Works*: Leipsic, vol. iii. p. 95, 1838).

For the abundant data recently brought to light touching Kant's relation to Swedenborg, including his direct allusions to Swedenborg and the unmistakable borrowings from him, see Kant's *Lectures on Psychology* in Carl du Prel's Edition: Leipsic, 1889; P. von Lind's Karri's *Mystische Weltanschauung*: Munich, 1892; Heinze's *Observations on the Lectures of 1790-91 on Rational Psychology* and on the Lectures on Metaphysics; in the *Abhandlungen der Sachsischen Gesellschaft der Wissenschaften*: Leipzig, 1894. For a full discussion of these see the Introduction

# SWEDENBORG

to Kant's *Dreams of a Spirit Seer,* translated by Emanuel
Goerwitz; Swan Sonnenschein & Co.: London, 1900.

But the "contemplation of the soul itself " was to come
to Swedenborg in quite another way, and his transition from the
attitude of the rigidly mechanical physicist and the speculative
philosopher to that of the illumined seer and the exponent of a
philosophy no longer human only, but angelic constitutes an
experience unique in the annals of human thought. It involves a
self-renunciation, a quenching of the loftiest ambitions of the
unaided human intellect, which is in itself tragic. The principle in
his philosophy of Discrete Degrees, viz. that the order of influx
is from within outward, from center to circumference, from the
spiritual to the natural, and not the reverse, was to claim for its
illustrious first martyr the author of these sublime researches,
who had boldly aspired to open all doors and force an access to
the soul itself through the avenues of natural experimental
knowledge. Not, however, as in Kant, was the quest to go for
ever unrewarded and be dogmatically proscribed. Swedenborg
claims that in himself a new kind of human, nay, even
experimental knowledge was granted to mankind.

Religion and a knowledge of the soul, of immortality and
of a spiritual world of objective substantiality were indeed to be
enjoyed within the "bounds of practical reason," but through
"things seen and heard," by the extraordinary opening of the
spiritual senses of a man to the experience of the unseen world of
spirit and all its realities, and to a rational understanding of the
laws of that world. It was in the year 1744, at the very time when
he was diligently pursuing his duties as Assessor in the College
of Mines, corresponding with the Academies of Science at Paris,
St. Petersburg and Stockholm, and contributing papers on
important civic and national questions in the House of Nobles of
the Swedish Parliament, that he heard, as he declares, in the
midst of his most ambitious researches into the nature of the
human body and of the soul itself, the voice of God bidding him

to lay down all his ambitious strivings in science, to close his great books the Principia, the Animal Kingdom, and the Soul, and to open one Book alone henceforth the Holy Scripture and seek there what, by a special, divine illumination, should be revealed to him as the Word of God in its internal and spiritual sense. The voice was reverently heard and obeyed. With awful interior struggles of soul, in which worldly and intellectual ambition fought with the impulse to this higher calling, nights and days passed in agony until at length, on an Easter Sunday in April 1744, he goes to the Holy Supper and hears the hymn, "Jesus is my best of friends," and on returning it seems to him "as if the buds had opened and were green." In the restless night that followed there came a feeling of holiest peace, "as if he were in heaven; and he can only cry out 'Holy, holy, holy, Lord God of Hosts! Praise and honor and glory be to the Highest!' Thenceforward he said, 'I accepted the following creed: God's will be done! I am Thine and not mine. God give His grace for this work, for it is not mine!'" (Doc. vol. ii. and pp. 164, 172).

Then comes the vaster journey, the greater exploration in which, at the call of his Maker, this spiritual Columbus explores the living spheres of the other world, beholds the structure, the laws, the life of heaven, the vast relation of correspondence existing between the spiritual and natural worlds, and the intimate and momentous relation between our present life and the future life for which it is shaping us, for good or for bad, in the world to come.

The change in Swedenborg's study from the science of nature to that of the spiritual world and of divine revelation is not without its parallels in the case of his great contemporaries Leibnitz and Newton, both of whom in their later period devoted themselves to theology and to the explanation of Scriptural prophecies. The remarkable feature of Swedenborg's case was that, while his spiritual quest involved the abnegation of all pride of invention or of creation, so that he ' was not permitted to be taught even by any angel, but by the Lord alone while reading the Word, still, the substructure of earthly science and philosophy by which he had climbed thus far, instead of being set aside as worthless, was found to be in its general form the exact material setting of the interior spiritual principles now to be revealed from above. That which was submissively renounced is thus restored tenfold, and in a glorified reality. The splendid system of psychology and physiology, and of the elementary world, is now found to be part of a stupendous series of sciences mutually corresponding and dependent, reaching even to the now revealed true knowledge of the soul, of the spiritual world, of heaven and the divine nature itself. It is the apotheosis of the human philosophy which had yielded its self-life upon the cross of the world's contempt. It was the beatification of the science which had sought to be the handmaid of the Lord, and which had uttered, in the final despair of human searching for the real knowledge, "be it unto me according to Thy Word!"

There are features of this self-renunciation of Swedenborg in the transition from his philosophical to his theological labors that have been but little appreciated by those who have formed a hasty estimate of his personality and his work. Of these the following may be here mentioned.

## a. THE CHANGE OF LITERARY STYLE

The classic elegance of his Latin style, which has elicited in his philosophical works the admiration of critics, and which in the mystic prose poem, *De Cultu et Amore Dei, de Ortu Primogeniti, et de Paradiso* (Londini: apud Kegan Paul, Trench et soc. (MDCCCLXXIII.))... a work written just at the transition period, reminds one of Dante in its grave simplicity and beauty of diction, now gives place to a mode of statement absolutely without ornament, following closely the English construction, as if with a view to that English reading public which, according to his own prophecy, was to be the central vehicle of the distribution of his teachings to the world. Thus, by way of comparison in style, Dante begins his great poem, the *Divina Comedia*, with these words:

Nel mezzo del cammin di nostra vita
Mi ritrovai per una selva oscura
Che la diritta via era smarrita.

In the midst of the journey of this life
I found myself in a dark forest
Where the straight way was lost.

Swedenborg begins thus his poem entitled, *The Worship and Love of God: the Birth of our Earth and of Paradise*:

Cum solus quondam in Luco urbano cogitationum turbas discutiendi gratio obambularem ac viderem viduari foliis arbores:

Walking once alone in a pleasant grove and observing that the trees were shedding their foliage... I reflected... on the vicissitudes of things.

Compare this with the bald simplicity and the English phrasing of the following, from the theological work *De Coelo et Inferno*:

*De Luce in Coelo*

Lux Coeli non est naturalis sicut mundi, sed est spiritualis; est enim a Domino ut sole et sol est Divinus Amor. Quod procedit a Domino ut Sole in Coelis vocatur Divinum Verum est tamen in essentia sua Divinum Bonum unitum Divino Vero: inde Angelis Lux et Calor; Ex Divino Vero est angelis Lux; et ex Divino Bono est illis Calor.

# SWEDENBORG

## b. THE SEER

For nineteen years since the beginning of those writings which claim to have been produced under supernatural illumination, the works appear anonymously, and for a long time their authorship is an entire secret. In 1768 the work on *Conjugal Love* bears the title Ab Emanele Swedenborgio, Sueco; and on the title-page of the great final summary *Vera Christiana Religio*, continent Universam Theologiam Novae Ecclesiae, published in 1771, appears the author's name with the words added: Domini Jesu Christi Servo, revealing the character in which he would henceforth be known in relation to these writings, namely, as a messenger of divine truths rather than as a leader in speculation. Still another remarkable phase of this laying down of a prior life of earthly learning, and the taking up of a life and learning given from above, was the entire absence therein of either the ascetic self-mortification or of the ecstatic trance which we associate in our minds with the oriental and medieval "illuminati." Nothing of this kind existed in Swedenborg's case. The life resumed was not only a healthy and vigorous one, with nothing suggestive of the visionary or fanatic, but in this stage of his literary activity appear the same logical order and clearness of reasoning, the same vastness and comprehensiveness of method, the same firm grasp of particulars under universal unities, which elicit our wonder in the philosophical works.

The splendid intellectual instrument polished for use by the discipline of the earlier period now seemed to have found its true and worthy field of application. In a subject-matter wholly new, the art and the skill are the same as before. The change of plane from material to spiritual realities produces no flaw, no yielding in the logic. The flippant assumption of lunacy and madness at this period of his writing is confronted with the majestic presence of a system of theology and of spiritual philosophy so perfect in its rational consistency, not only with itself, but with the other realms of knowledge, that for this very cause some have been led to call it "too logical a system to be revealed." Utterly as the human philosopher had subjected his rational faculties to the employment of the divine Master in communicating to men through his understanding the "Wisdom of Angels," it was not by the sacrifice of reason but by its illumination and inspiration from the Author of reason itself that this new light was given. The man who was "daily in intercourse with angels," who was writing the "Heavenly Secrets" of the Holy Scripture, and Claimed to be witnessing the awful scenes of a "Last Judgment" in the World of Spirits preparatory to the introduction of a new age of the world, so far from being a dazed and dreamy mystic or a recluse from society, as so many have ignorantly assumed, was in the very years of such employment the warm personal and political friend of the then Prime Minister of Sweden, Count Andrew von Hopken, and was taking a very active part in the deliberations of the Swedish Diet.

Thus in the year 1760, in which he writes his treatise on the "Last Judgment," and "On the Spiritual World;" the year in which it became first publicly known that he was the author of *Arcana Caelestia*, he presents to the Diet the following papers:

"Memorial in favor of a return to the Pure Metallic Currency", "Additional Considerations with respect to the Course of Exchange", "Memorial to the King against the Exportation of Copper", "Memorial declining to become a member of the Private Commission on Exchange."

In 1761, the year of Swedenborg's memorable announcement of the "Queen's Secret," and of the discovery of the "lost receipt" for Mme. de Marteville events which so aroused the wonder of Kant when verified by him beyond the possibility of doubt (see Kant's letter to Fraulein von Knobloch), Swedenborg presents to the Diet a "Memorial on the

Maintenance of the Country and the Preservation of its Freedom," and conducts a political contest with Councilor Nordencrantz in defense of the Swedish Government. (Count Hopken, the Prime Minister of Sweden, who had known Swedenborg intimately during the long period of the twenty-seven years of his professed continuous experience of open intercourse with the spiritual world, testifies that in the year 1761, which was in the midst of Swedenborg's other-world experiences, the ablest papers submitted to the Diet of Sweden on matters of national finance were those of Swedenborg, sitting as a member of the House of Nobles.)

Such is the normal character of a man living in two worlds and performing conscientiously his functions in both. His self-renunciation was not that of the monk or quietist: it was simply that of a man whose understanding, trained in all the learning of earth, was willing to be employed in conveying a supernatural knowledge rather than in presenting speculations of his own on things that transcend the human senses. The crucial test of the kind of intellectual self-renunciation which Swedenborg attained -is one which few of his contemporaries in the ranks of speculative philosophy, and few of those who would fain be his followers and admirers on the natural plane, have been able to sustain. Kant was sufficiently attracted by his claim of a specially illumined reason to feel that he must remain either to worship or to scoff. He chose the latter; but in doing so he had to divest the object of his mirth of the garments of the seer and clothe him in the mask of the harlequin a mask which the sober reason of subsequent time has been less and less willing to accept. In representing Swedenborg as the arch medium of the spiritists and writing under his name a treatise of Spiritism, (Kant's *Traume eines Geistersehers*. Reclam. Leipsic.) Kant chooses to fight a man of straw, rather than to assail principles of truth which, as he is driven elsewhere to acknowledge, "bear a striking resemblance to his own." The true relation of Swedenborg to the Spiritism whether of Kant or of the present time can best be seen by the following statements from his own writings.

### c. SWEDENBORG NOT A MEDIUM

"It is believed by many that they may be taught by the Lord by spirits speaking with them; but they do not know that this is fraught with danger to their souls. As soon as spirits begin to speak with man, they come out of their spiritual state into the natural state of man, they join themselves with the thoughts of his affection, and from these they speak with him. The Pythonists of old were such, and also the Magi in Egypt and Babylon. Thus the worship of God was turned into the worship of demons, and the church perished. Therefore such intercourse was forbidden the children of Israel under penalty of death." (*Apocalypse Explained*, 1182).

While Swedenborg claims to have had intromission into the spiritual world an experience not to be confounded with the admission of spirits from that world into this yet he disclaims entirely any office of mediumship whereby spirits spoke or acted through him, in communicating truth from the other world.

"I have had discourse with spirits and angels now for several years, and no spirit has dared, nor has any angel desired, to tell me anything, much less to instruct me in regard to anything of the Word, or of doctrine from the Word; but the Lord alone has taught me." (*Divine Providence*, 135).

"From the first day I have never received anything of the doctrines from any angel, but from the Lord alone while I was reading the Word." (*True Christian Religion*, 779).

"At this day, revelation is only made by means of the Word" (*Arcana Coelestia*, 10355).

# SWEDENBORG

Emerson, in a later day, enchanted the newly awakened Puritan mind with beautiful glimpses of spiritual verities and universal ideas directly traceable to the influence of Swedenborg whom as a natural philosopher he cannot too highly extol; but the delights of intellectual creation were too dear to Emerson to allow him to accept the dictates of a direct revelation, and his only resource is to treat lightly the spiritual receptivity in another mind of which his own nature was incapable. "Sandy deserts" he calls now those honest and prosaic narrations and definitions of spiritual phenomena which the seer, for whom rhetoric has lost all value, deals out with tiresome repetition; forgetting that he has unconsciously absorbed from this homely and despised source the spiritual content of his own ideality and ethics. It is this, clothed with his own oracular brilliancy, that Emerson has handed down as the chief heritage of what is known as the New England Transcendentalism.

Its message, above all, is that of man's immediate environment in a world whose substance is superior to matter, but related to it as a man's soul to his body. To take from Emerson Swedenborg's doctrine of Correspondence would leave much of his writing dull and dark. (See Article, "Swedenborg," by Francis Hedge, Christian Examiner, November 1833; Article in New Jerusalem Magazine, Boston, November 1893; Emerson's "Essay on Poetry and Imagination" in *Letters and Social Aims*.)

It was during the years of transition (1743-45) that Swedenborg wrote two works which reveal unmistakably the trend his mind was following, as anticipating a goal ahead whose real significance he could not yet comprehend. One of these is the *Adversaria,* a book of notes upon the Old Testament for his own use, in compiling which, and by a study of the original texts, he acquired a minute knowledge of the letter of the Scriptures, with some glimpses of an historical-allegorical sense to form a kind of basis of his later strictly spiritual interpretation.

# SWEDENBORG

The other transitional work was *The Worship and Love of God*, treating of the Birth of the Earth, Paradise and the Abode of Living Creatures; also of the Nativity, Infancy and Love of the First-begotten, or Adam (*De Cultu et Amore Dei*, etc.). The style of the work is that of a prose poem. It might be called a drama of Creation, in which figure the various orders of the intelligences and loves of the human soul moving upon a background of the world's elemental activity in evolving a cosmos. As a theory of evolution, in its splendid audacity it puts the more modern theories which pass by that name quite into insignificance. The language is graceful and elegant, suggesting reminiscences of the author's early studies of the Metamorphoses of Ovid. There is no claim in it of supernatural knowledge, the purpose being avowedly to study the Biblical narrative of Creation in the light of a scientific cosmogony and psychology and purely "according to the thread of reason." (For a full account of this remarkable work and an attempt at its interpretation see the Essay, "A Drama of Creation" in *The New Metaphysics*,. by Frank Sewall. London: J.. Spiers. 1887.)

A description of the formation of our planet out of the sun in the bursting forth of worlds out of its womb and their projection into the whirling spheres, is followed by that of its finding its true orbit and the fixing of temperatures and of seasons and the successive production of vegetable and animal life, and, at last, of the human creature; each of these orders being truly evolved from the one below, but immediately and successively, the transition being not from the highest vegetable to the lowest animal, but from the highest vegetable to the highest animal; so that man is born from the fruit of the tree in which all the finest essences of nature are centered and combined and which grows in the midst of the earthly Paradise. Nowhere else does the author speak of this theory of the origin of man. It seems as if it were the poetic capstone to the system of combined physics and metaphysics which had occupied his mind for so many years, but one which was, by an abrupt lifting of the curtain, to give place to a vision no longer of the phenomenal and theoretical but the real, the immortal and the eternal the true knowledge of the spirit and of the spiritual world.

## d. THE SPIRITUAL DIARY

In this *Spiritual Diary*, an immense body of memoranda written during the years 1747-52, Swedenborg describes with prosaic exactness the new world opened to his vision, the places visited, the characters met, the conversations held in the spiritual world.

The most startling and wonderful scenes are here related, in the matter-of-fact manner of everyday occurrences. The entries in this purely private record, published from the Latin MSS. in 1844, number over 5,500, and they constitute, with their careful analysis of characters and situations, a storehouse of spiritual data of an entirely unique value. The following extract will serve as a sample of these entries, and will at the same time throw light upon the problems of modern hypnotism, spiritism, telepathy, and like experiences.

*Self-Delusion of Spirits.* "It has been shown to me many times that spirits who spoke with me imagined that they were the men I was thinking of; nor did other spirits know otherwise. For instance, yesterday and today, one of them was so much like a person known to me in life, in everything (so far as I knew) pertaining to him, that nothing could be more like. Wherefore, let those who speak with spirits beware when spirits say that they are persons who are known to them, and that they are the dead. For there are classes of spirits of a similar nature. When accordant things are called forth in the memory of a man and are thus represented to them, they suppose that they are the identical person about whom he is thinking; then, all the things representing the person thought of are called forth from the memory, even the words, speech, tones of voice, gestures, and many other things." (Aug. 18, 1748).

*Concerning the Lord's Prayer.* "When the Lord's Prayer, which comprehends all celestial and spiritual things, is read, there may be infused into each particular so many things that heaven itself shall not be capable of comprehending them, and that, too, according to the capacity and use of every one. The more internally and intimately any one penetrates, the more fully or abundantly the things of heaven are understood; by those in lower states they are not comprehended but are a kind of arcana to them, some being ineffable. Celestial ideas which all emanate from the Lord, the lower they descend, or the lower the character of the men to whom they come, the more complete appears the closing up of the mind, till at length a certain hardness ensues in which there is little or nothing besides the sense of the letter or the ideas conveyed by the words; whence it was given to know, from the Lord's Prayer, what kind of souls they had been in the life of the body as to the doctrine of their faith, inasmuch as it was granted to them to have their former sense of these things when offering prayer (April 1, 1748). Thus it is that the idea expands upwards or inwards from corporeal things, and indeed to indefinite extent in every degree, or, in other words, through indefinitely multiplied expansions in the interiors of the mind, and so in the more interior parts, and in the inmosts."

At length with the first volume of the *Arcana Coelestia*, written in the full and certain light of the new revelation, Swedenborg begins those remarkable treatises in which he publicly claims to set forth, for the enlightenment of the whole Christian world, the truths of a supernatural and divine origin by the divine mercy revealed to him. The Arcana itself is a work in Latin in twelve volumes, and consists of an exposition of the internal and spiritual sense of the books of Genesis and Exodus.

## CHAPTER V: THE THEOLOGICAL WRITINGS

### 1749-1772

Interspersed between the chapters of the Arcana are treatises on various phenomena of the spiritual world and statements of "heavenly doctrine." The publication of this stupendous work, begun in London in 1749, covered a period of seven years. The handsome quarto volumes, as they appeared anonymously from time to time, were mainly distributed in gifts to the bishops and to the leading universities of England and the Continent. Whatever funds accrued from their sale were devoted to the British Society for the Propagation of the Gospel. After this initial work appear in succession at short intervals, for a period of fifteen years, the following treatises: In 1768: *Heaven and Hell*; also the *Intermediate World, or World of Spirits. A Relation of Things Heard and Seen.*

*The Last Judgment and the Destruction of Babylon*: showing that all the Predictions in the Revelation are at this day fulfilled: being a Revelation of Things Heard and Seen.

*On The White Horse* mentioned in the Revelation, ch. xix., with particulars respecting the Word and its Spiritual Sense; extracted from the Arcana Coelestia.

*On The Earths in our Solar System* and the Earths in the Starry Heavens, with an account of their Inhabitants and also of the Spirits and Angels there.

*On The New Jerusalem and its Heavenly Doctrines* according to what has been heard from Heaven; to which is prefixed information regarding the New Heaven and the New Earth.

# SWEDENBORG

In 1763 appear *Angelic Wisdom (Sapientia Angelica)*, concerning the Divine Love and Wisdom, and the *Four Leading Doctrines of the New Church signified by the New Jerusalem in the Revelation*, being those respecting *the Lord, the Sacred Scripture, Faith and Life.*

In 1764: *Angelic Wisdom* concerning the Divine Providence.

In 1766: *The Apocalypse Revealed*, in which are disclosed the Arcana therein foretold.

In 1768: *Conjugal Love and its Chaste Delights*; also Adulterous Love and its Insane Pleasures.

In 1769: *A Brief Exposition of the Doctrine of the New Church* signified by the New Jerusalem in the Revelation. Also *The Intercourse between the Soul and the Body.*

Finally in 1771 appears the great summary of his system, *The True Christian Religion; containing the Universal Theology of the New Church, foretold in Daniel* vii. 13, 14, and in the Apocalypse xxi. 1, 2.

In this work we have a complete body of theology systematically presented, proceeding from a profound discussion of Absolute Being to the doctrine of the Lord the Redeemer, the Holy Spirit and the Divine Trinity; the Sacred Scripture; the Catechism, or Decalogue, explained as to its External and Internal Sense; Faith, Charity, Free Determination; Repentance, Reformation and Regeneration; Imputation, Baptism, the Holy Supper; the Consummation of the Age, the Coming of the Lord and the New Heaven and the New Church.

The chapters of this work, like those of the Arcana, are interspersed with Memorabilia, or accounts of the author's personal observations and conversations in the spiritual world, embracing visions in the heavens and in the hells, remarkable pictures of a Dantesque simplicity and strength without the least indication of poetic fancy or rhetorical effort. They are relations of "things heard and seen" by a traveler returned from a hitherto unknown land. Bizarre and uncouth as many of the scenes depicted are, being all of them phenomena appearing according to the universal law of spontaneous symbolic representation which prevails in that world, they have their nearest parallels in the prophetic visions contained in the Holy Scriptures, and when carefully analyzed are found to be only the rational embodiments, or *Darstellung*, of spiritual states and relations actually existing. In these narratives figure spirits who had been inhabitants of other planets. Scenes are portrayed as occurring in the Last Judgment, the great *Aufklarung* in the world of spirits where were taking place those moral changes from an old to a new age, which, from the beginning of the French Revolution until now, have been taking form on earth in the transformation of all things political, economical and religious. All these narrations will bear the closest rational scrutiny as to their credibility, provided the single premise be granted that the other world exists. So consistent, so realistic indeed are they that the reader is compelled to admit that these very experiences, instead of being extraordinary and fanciful, are the things most natural and likely to occur provided there be a sphere of spiritual causes behind the shifting scenes of the drama of our life here.

*A Memorable Relation.* "Awaking one morning from sleep, I saw two angels descending from heaven, one from the southern quarter and the other from the eastern, each in his chariot drawn by white horses. The chariot of the angel from the southern quarter shone like silver, and that of the angel of the eastern quarter like gold, and the reins which they held in their hands glowed with a flaming light like the dawn of day. These two angels appeared thus to me when at a distance, but when they came near they did not appear in chariots, but in their own angelic human form. The one from the eastern quarter of heaven was clad in bright purple raiment, and the one from the southern quarter in raiment of a violet blue. As soon as they reached the inferior regions below the heavens they ran to meet each other, as if they strove which should be first, and mutually embraced and kissed each other. I was informed that these two angels, during their abode on earth, had been conjoined in the bond of an interior friendship, but that now one was in the eastern heaven and the other in the southern; in the eastern heaven are those who are in love from the Lord, and in the southern heaven those who are in wisdom from the Lord. When they had conversed together some time about the magnificent objects and scenery in their respective heavens, they entered upon the discussion of this question: whether heaven, in its essence, be love or wisdom. In this they agreed that the one derived its origin from the other; but the debate was which was the primitive and which the derivative."

"The angel from the southern heaven then asked the other, 'What is love?' to which he replied; 'Love originating from the Lord as a sun is the vital heat of angels and men, consequently the ease of their life; and the derivations of love are called affections, and by them are produced perceptions, and thus thoughts, whence it follows that wisdom in its origin is love, consequently that thought, in its origin, is the affection of that love; and it is evident, from the derivations examined in their order, that thought is only the form of affection. The reason why this is not known is, because thoughts are in light and affections in heat, so that the mind reflects upon its thoughts, but not on its affections. That thought is only the form of the affection of some particular love may also be illustrated by the case of speech, which is only the form of sound; which is a just illustration, because sound corresponds with affection, and speech with thought; therefore affection forms the sound or tone of the voice, and thought the speech or words of a discourse. This may be further elucidated by this consideration, that if you take away sound from speech, nothing of speech remains; and in like manner if you take away affection from thought, nothing of thought remains. Hence, then, it is plain that love is the all of wisdom; consequently the essence of the heavens is love and their existence is wisdom; or, what is the same thing, the heavens have their being from the divine love and exist from the divine love by the divine wisdom; therefore, as was said above, the one derives its origin from the other..."

"The angels conversed on these subjects spiritually, and spiritual discourse contains and infolds in it thousands of things which natural language cannot express, and, what is wonderful, such as do not so much as fall within the ideas of natural thought. After conversing together for some time on these and similar subjects the angels departed, and, as they retired to their respective heavens, their heads appeared encompassed with stars, and when they were removed to a distance from me, they again appeared in chariots as before."

## CLASSIFICATION OF THE THEOLOGICAL WORKS

The treatises on Theology, like those on Philosophy, may be classified in three divisions: the Analytic, the Synthetic and the Doctrinal.

The first, the Analytic, embraces the record of things heard and seen in the spiritual world, and the particulars of truth revealed in the internal sense of the Scriptures. Here belong the *Arcana,* The *Apocalypse Revealed, Heaven and Hell, The Last Judgment, The Earths in the Universe,* and *The Memorabilia* interspersed through all the works.

The Synthetic class embraces those which contain the laws governing all spiritual phenomena and Divine operations, and the relation of matter to spirit, or of the two worlds. These are the *Angelic Wisdom concerning the Divine Love and*

*Wisdom,* and *Concerning the Divine Providence*, and the work on *Influx.*

The Doctrinal class, in which, from all these particulars and summaries, a complete system of theology and ethics is evolved, forming the final and perfected form of Christianity, that of a New Universal Church. Here are to be named *The True Christian Religion, The Four Leading Doctrines*, and *The New Jerusalem and its Heavenly Doctrines*.

For a discussion of the loftiest and most sacred relation of human life, that upon which the whole social economy must rest or go asunder the marriage relation the reader will resort to the work on *Conjugal Love and its Chaste Delights*, in which the complementary relation of the sexes is shown to be mental as well as physical, and hence having a significance beyond the earthly life. The twofold nature of the human mind in will and intellect, patterned as "the image of God," after the union of love and wisdom in the divine nature, finds its ultimate expression in both the mental and physical differences of the two sexes. Their union in marriage constitutes the complete man; and from its origin in the Divine Itself the marriage union is essentially chaste and holy. Swedenborg calls it "the precious jewel of human life and the repository of the Christian religion." Every violation and perversion of this relation of the sexes he designates as evil, and as such forbidden in the *Decalogue.* Especially and definitely does he make this assertion in the work entitled "The Doctrine of Life for the New Jerusalem" in treating of the Commandment regarding adultery (Nos. 74-9); while in an Appendix to Conjugal Love on *Scortatory Love and its Insane Pleasures*, the reverse of the heavenly order is shown, together with the provisions by which, in the disordered moral conditions of society, sexual evils may be mitigated and some capacity for true marriage preserved.

Pervading all the writings of this period is a complete

system of Ethics based upon the law of Use, or of Mutual Service, which law pervades the universe throughout from its very constitution and exhibits that ladder by which all created things are conjoined to God, their Creator. Social economics are treated in the little work on Charity. This is defined, not as meaning mere benevolence or alms-giving, but as the faithful pursuance by every man of the duties of his own office in society, together with the shunning of all evils as sins against God. In this doctrine man is represented as a "form of charity," or as that moral and free instrument through which the universal love of God the Creator can be dispensed among men in their doing of useful service and in their happiness realized in this doing. Neither the good nor the happiness is man's own; but it flows down from God into those channels of useful, neighborly living which a truly organized society provides; and man's entire share in the doing and the blessing consists in his removing from his motives and his acts those evils of self-love which are opposed to the inflow of the divine Altruism. The little work on Charity discusses the relation of the individual to the common good, and what conduct constitutes charity in the Ruler, the Magistrate, the Priest, the Soldier, the Servant and other offices. On its largest scale Swedenborg's system of social order is displayed in his doctrine of the Grand Man (*Maximus Homo*), in which Society as a whole or the Kingdom of God is represented as forming an organic unit patterned after the human form and so in the image of God. Thus it reflects the perfections of the Creator who is essential love, on the plane of the infinite relations and uses of men in their several capacities for loving and serving the neighbor.

The work on The Earths in the Universe brings in an important phase of this doctrine, showing how the inhabitants of the several planets by their distinct moral qualities, go to make up the completeness in the spiritual world of the great Social Man.

## THE NEW AGE

The distinctive character of the New Age is the return to a rational unity in man's conception of God, of the Universe and of Life; in the conception of God as the unity of the three essentials of personality in the Divine Humanity of Jesus Christ glorified, the one Lord God of Heaven and Earth; in the conception of the unity of the Universe through the influx of One life in the three degrees God, Spirit, and Nature which are one, not by confusion, but by correspondence; and in the conception of the unity of Life by the restored unity of faith in God with charity to the neighbor. Swedenborg, on being asked to explain his theology, replied, "There are two principles of it that God is One, and that there is a conjunction of Charity and Faith."

## CHAPTER VI: PHILOSOPHY AND THE SAPIENTIA ANGELICA

Of the twofold series of Swedenborg's writings, the Scientific and the Theological, we have as a unique result a complete *Weltanschauung*, or World-system, which embraces in harmonious and strictly logical accord the two worlds of human experience, the natural and the spiritual. Probably no such a complete survey of the whole realm of Being in a scientific form has ever been presented to rational contemplation. Not to mention the open conflict between science and revelation which from time immemorial has been looked at as belonging necessarily to the existing order of things, the attempts towards a harmony hitherto essayed have reduced themselves without exception either into the mystic's acceptance of the transcendental knowledge, together with his abandonment of natural learning as illusory and worthless; or into the denial of any real knowledge beyond the natural, and the consequent regarding of ideas of God of the soul, its freedom and immortality as pious fictions of the practical reason, the necessary postulates of man's ethical nature, but merely human in their origin, and subject to all the limitations of the human mind. For the first time appears a man who claims to have beheld with twofold vision the twofold universe, and whose understanding, in its unshaken integrity and steady grasp, has taken in the laws and relations of both spheres, and, ignoring and despising neither, has combined the laws and phenomena of the two worlds in a perfect system.

This is Swedenborg's unique position in the history of human thought. He has presented to the world a system of Universal Philosophy based in its spiritual as well as its natural contents on analytic and experimental knowledge. "Being asked," says Swedenborg, "how from a philosopher I became a theologian, I answered, 'In the same manner that fishers were made disciples and apostles by the Lord'; and that I also, from early youth, had been a spiritual fisherman! On hearing this, the inquirer asked what a spiritual fisherman was. I replied that a fisher, in the spiritual sense of the Word, signifies a man who investigates and teaches natural truths, and afterwards spiritual truths, in a rational manner; for the latter are founded upon the former." (*Influx*, 20)

It is a positive transcendentalism in that it is a knowledge transcending the senses of the physical body, but real to those organs of the spiritual body which in every man become released into conscious activity at death, and in extraordinary instances enjoy this activity even in this world. The two great fields of research in all their distinctiveness claim each its period of exhaustive development. "Philosophy" is the term which Swedenborg applies to the kind of research employed in the first of these fields. The term is used in the sense of the natural philosophy of his day, as the survey of nature, whether in the physical or psychological fields, as a grand mechanism, subject everywhere to the laws discoverable in geometry, physics and mechanics. Only he adheres to that element as essential which he calls the soul; and while he confesses that his cosmogony reduces itself to a perfect mechanism so absolute and universal is the sway of physical law in nature still the presence of this supernatural fact must everywhere be conceded. "I have no objection," he says, "to my system of the world being called mechanism, only let it be an animated mechanism." This pursuit of the soul throughout the first period is therefore always within the limits of a time-and-space world. He sought its first essence in the fiber and animal spirit, just as in physics he sought his initial atom in the point and the first finite.

The conception of God throughout the philosophic period is that of the Infinite as the requisite source of initial motion, the idea of an infinite personality and of a divine humanity being as yet but dimly conceived. All this becomes changed in the second period. The philosophy of the first period now gives way to the Sapientia Angelica, which term we must take to mean, not the particular knowledge of a superior kind which the angels possess and can impart to each other and to men, but the kind of knowledge of which the human soul becomes capable when translated into a world above time and space and where the very elements are spiritual, the sun of that world being itself the first effulgence of the infinite love and wisdom of God, and, consequently, the very atmospheres, and the heat and light conveyed in them, being tremulous waves of substantial good and truth. The Sapientia Angelica, hence, is a knowledge of spiritual realities or of those truly vital substances and forces which go to furnish the great mechanism of nature with a soul. It is the actual vision and touch of a world of spiritual substance which the purified human spirit is capable of experiencing after rising out of the world of symbolic material phenomena by putting off the material body with its senses.

Rarely, if ever, does Swedenborg employ the term "philosophy" in reference to this immediate angelic experience, which he calls "wisdom." He uses this term intentionally in distinction from knowledge or intelligence, the first of these being, in his definition, applied to the acquiring of information through the senses and their environment; the second, to the orderly arrangement of these acquired knowledges in their respective groups by means of the rational faculty; the third, the wisdom itself, being the truth acquired now seen and loved truly, in its own nature and worth, as the form of good. Wisdom, therefore, while resting upon knowledge and reason, yet is a distinct kind of immediate perception which the purified spirit enjoys after death in the degree in which, in his own experience, the truth has become the form of his action from his very love of it as the form of good. It is not to be identified with the Gnostic's or the theosophist's immediate vision of the truth as a state above and apart from voluntary and intellectual activity. In wisdom the *proprium*, or the personality of the angel, is realized in its most intense form. If it were not so this angelic contemplation of reality would fail of its purpose in the divine scheme of the round of uses. The angelic contemplation of reality comes from the shining of a real heavenly light in the mind.

Can there, now, be any comprehensive philosophy of Swedenborg, strictly speaking? We answer Yes, for the two reasons that there are certain fundamental constructive laws that characterize alike both systems, the natural and the spiritual, and that accordingly the two worlds and their respective cosmogonies are brought visibly into their relation of a perfect correspondence. The harmony of the two systems can only be attributed to their being constructed according to a common organum, or method.

## SWEDENBORG'S *NOVUM ORGANUM*

This truly new *organum*, which constitutes Swedenborg's great contribution to philosophy, is his doctrine of Influx, of Discrete Degrees and their Correspondence. The world is vibration, action, and reaction. The Universe is the theater of altruistic love. Force originates in will, and the primal will is the Divine Love. Life is love emanating by wisdom into created spheres, and there operating in uses. These spheres are not a continuous plane, but are in discrete degrees, and related by correspondence.

These discrete degrees are, in their eternal divine potential nature, Love, Wisdom and Use; in their cosmological functions, End, Cause and Effect; in theology, God, Spirit and the Natural World; in revelation they are given the names of a holy Trinity Father, Son and Holy Spirit. In ontological terms they become Substance, Form and Thing; in philosophy, the Real, the Ideal and the Actual; in psychology, the Will, the Intellect and Action; in speech, Affection, Thought and Utterance; in the building of language, the Vowel, the Consonant

and the Word; the Verb, the Subject and the Predicate. In all
these trines, which cover with sufficient completeness the whole
realm of being and activity, there will be found the invariable
presence of these three essentials, which are necessary to the
being of anything that exists or can be conceived of as existing;
namely, the why, or the purpose for which it exists, which
Swedenborg calls the End; the how, or the manner and law by
which it exists, called by Swedenborg Cause (meaning the
instrumental cause or, *causa efficiens*, in distinction from the
end as the *causa finalis*), and finally the resultant thing, the what,
or that which Swedenborg calls the Effect. These three are
discrete because they are, by the very nature of things,
intransmutable.

One may reside within and actuate, the other, but without
ever becoming that other. Will may prompt the intellect, and put
on a form or determination in the intellect, and both these may
become actual in a word or deed of the body. But will is not
intellect, nor is intellect action. They are for ever discrete in their
nature, however one may operate through another, and so all
become embodied in the ultimate what, or thing. These
fundamental distinctions, existing eternally in the very order of
the world when strictly observed, forbid the confusion of
substance between spirit and matter and between God and
nature, and so render possible a conception of the immanence of
God in nature which is free from Pantheism, or the confusion of
God with nature.

These "discrete degrees," thus distinguished by
Swedenborg from "continuous degrees," or the ordinary degrees
of comparison which mean merely more or less of the same
quality, are thus essentially constructive degrees; they are
productive, even dynamic in character, as they imply the action
of one force through various media under a fixed law. The force
is life itself; the media are the series, orders and degrees through
which life descends from its source to its ultimates; the descent

itself is influx; and the law of relation and adaptation by which the descent is possible is the law of Correspondence.

It is by virtue of correspondence that thought can express itself in the definite form of airwaves we call a word the two orders of existence being in themselves utterly discrete. So the mind finds its utterance or activity in the body, and the whole spiritual world its expression and its symbol in the whole physical universe. There is no confusion of substance even by means of the finest electron. The two worlds are absolutely discrete in nature, but they communicate by a perfect correspondence. The eye itself is formed in correspondence with the nature of the ether vibrations which reach it, and so is capable of transmitting, not the ether, but its motions in the substance of the nerves and fibers of vision and so to the seats of sensation. Here these motions are again taken up by the vessels of the mind in the soul's vision, imagination, thought and determination, from which begins the reaction through the motor nerves. There is no interfusion of matter and thought. There is a series and order of degrees, and there is a correspondence, and so an influx of motion and of force.

Viewed under the same law, the cosmos is a system of spheres emanating from the infinite Divine. The same law which governs the series God, the Spiritual Word and Nature, controls the relation of the successive atmospheres aura, ether, atmospheric air. The same trinal series is visible in the succession of forms vortical, spiral, circular in the formation of the material atom. It is the transmission of one force by vibratory motion through various media that constitutes what is known as the transmutation of energy. The various planes of the human mind, volitional, intellectual and sensuous, constitute the same trinal series, and so in consequence the same trinal division of the angelic heavens. Of these the highest, or celestial, is characterized by the spontaneity of love, the second or spiritual by the guidance of faith, and the lowest by the simple will to obey and to serve the power from above. In this universal world-view, the all of being is brought into the unity of the trinal One; not by confusion of substance but by influx, degrees and thus correspondence. So vast is this extension of the law of Discrete Degrees when seen to govern the spiritual as well as the natural world, that Swedenborg speaks of it, in his later period, as something hitherto unknown. In its natural scope he had indeed applied this law during the earlier period, and had been guided by it in all his researches. In his Principia he develops a world through the three degrees of Finites, Actives and Elementaries. In the Soul he describes the effect by contiguity, and the transmission, by vibration, of the ether rays upon the eye, of the eye upon the nerve, of the nerve upon the brain, of the brain upon the imagination, of the imagination upon the intellect, of the intellect upon the soul all by virtue of the perfect correspondence of each of these subtle media with the force communicated. But it was only the greater vision of the later illumination that enabled Swedenborg to see the same law operating in the action of God upon the spiritual world, and of the spiritual world upon nature. These entities are nowhere interfused or blended into a pantheistic mass, but for ever exist in their discrete degrees, eternally distinct, but one by perfect correspondence and harmonious interaction. Hence we may denominate Swedenborg's philosophic system as that of a Trinal Monism.

Without these three, End, Cause and Effect, nothing is, whether we speak of universal Being or the least existing thing. Each degree constitutes a plane of being by itself; it never becomes the other in its own series by any blending or continuity. It is in the other and actuates it, but never becomes the other. The End is in the mediate or Cause, and through this in the Effect or the thing ultimated.

Effect is not continuous with cause, as mere Cause intensified, nor is Cause intensified End. God is in all spiritual things without losing Himself in them by confusion with them. Spirit is in all nature and in all matter, giving it its form and all its force, without itself becoming matter, or matter by any process of refinement ever becoming spirit. Just as a man's will is in his thought, and both are in the spoken or written word, yet the word is not thought, and the thought itself is not will; but the three are one in the utterance, without confusion of substance. So is God in His going forth: is in all things and the Source of all things, and yet these things are not Himself.

In order that each lower degree may be the form and expression of the higher, it must perfectly correspond. Hence the Law of Correspondence is the correlative of the Law of Discrete Degrees. According to it each thing in nature corresponds to something in a co-existing spiritual world, which is the world of causes inasmuch as it is only in mind or spirit that relations have a real existence and hence that design and direction are possible. Only mind can do this. And finally, all things in the spiritual world have their real being in those particular ends in the Divine Love from which they are created.

## THE LAW OF CORRESPONDENCE APPLIED TO THE INTERPRETATION OF THE SCRIPTURES

The application of the Law of Correspondence to the interpretation of Holy Scripture as actual Divine revelation becomes manifest. As everything in nature has a Divine end and a spiritual meaning, so Divine revelation, expressed in terms taken from nature and from the thoughts and images of the human mind, becomes rationally conceivable. For the mind can conceive of the Divine Spirit selecting, by inspiration in the mind of the amanuensis, out of the vocabulary not only of nature but of human history and  tradition, those things, countries, persons and events which may be the outward form and symbols of inner, spiritual realities.

So may God "open His mouth in parables" and make known "by things that are made the things invisible, even His eternal power and God-head."

Applied to the conception of God and the Divine Trinity, the law of Discrete Degrees distinguishes the Father as the Ease, the Divine Love and primal Substance from the Son as the Ezistere, the Wisdom or Word by whom all things are, and from the Holy Spirit as that proceeding and perpetual Operation of the Divine Love and Wisdom in uses in the created world. It is in the sending forth of the Divine that things are created. Potentially existing from eternity as Love, Wisdom and Use in the one God, Jehovah, the Trinity becomes actual in time in the Divine Humanity of Jesus Christ. In the Word made Flesh the Divine Love, which is the Father, is made manifest, and through this the Holy Spirit is breathed upon the world. Thus in Him, Jesus Christ, "dwelleth all the fullness of the Godhead bodily."

The Divine Trinity is not a trinity of persons, but of person. The essential trinity of love, wisdom and their operation, or of will, thought and work, constitute personality whether human or divine. In the work of redemption Jehovah has clothed Himself in the womb of a virgin with the nature of man, and thus in the person of Jesus Christ taken upon Himself the burden of all the accumulated sinful heredity of mankind from the beginning. In the life of Jesus Christ on earth the Divine fought with those evils admitted into the infirm humanity by temptation and conquered them. By so doing He overcame the hells and subdued them unto Himself, and was enabled with the cry upon the cross. "It is finished," to say to all men "Be of good cheer. I have overcome the world."

Redemption therefore consisted, not in a plan of judicature by which divine justice was to be satisfied by a vicarious sacrifice, but it is a veritable *fait accompli*, a most real warfare with and victory over the hells, achieved by the one

# SWEDENBORG

Champion of human spiritual liberty.

This liberty is attainable by men through faith and obedience, not as conditions arbitrarily imposed, but as essential to that free self-activity on man's part, which enables him to become a voluntary recipient of God's love, and a willing subject of His Kingdom. The worship of Jesus Christ in His Divine Humanity as the one and only God of heaven and earth, and the one and only Savior of mankind, is therefore the corner stone of Swedenborg's religious system and of the doctrine which he outlined of a New Christianity. Swedenborg's religious scheme knows nothing of sect or nationality as affecting the Divine regard for man. All nations, and all religions are embraced under the survey of the Divine Providence, which looks to eternal ends, and strives to lift men continually out of the evil into which they have fallen through the abuse of their moral freedom, and to bring them into the liberty of heaven.

Since God in Jesus Christ is alone worshiped in all the heavens, all men of all religions who have believed and worshiped, however blindly and grossly here, will, in the intermediate World of Spirits, have the veils of heredity and local ignorance removed, and come to see the one true God behind all the various symbols by which He has been worshiped here. The only essential conditions of salvation are belief in the Divine and voluntary self-subjection to the Divine Law because it is Divine. Swedenborg's religion is eminently ethical and practical. According to him the "Kingdom of Heaven is a kingdom of uses." "All religion," he says, "is of life, and the life of religion is to do good." But by doing good is not meant eleemosynary acts of benevolence of the works of piety. It is rather the shunning of evils as sins against God, and the faithful performance of the duties of one's station from a religious motive. This constitutes the essence of Charity in the sublime sense in which Swedenborg uses this much-abused word. Charity is simply the love of God to man exercised by means of, or through, voluntary human agents. Men, by shunning evils as sins, open the channels of their life for the influx from above, and the outflow to their fellow-man of this universal divine benevolence and its delights. The universe is love; but love requires human moral freedom as the condition of its own exercise. When sinful self-love is removed by man, all the works that he performs become good works, and all earthly uses become the ultimate forms in which the ends of Divine love are realized in effect.

## THE SPIRITUAL HISTORY OF THE WORLD

As life is essentially love, so a man's life is what his love is; his intellect and his thoughts are the servants of this master, and the spiritual body is his immortal sensuous organism, adapted to uses in a world whose atmospheres are spiritual. Death is therefore but a cessation of consciousness in the material plane or degree, when the body, through injury or decay, ceases to respond to the vibrations or influx of the spiritual life. By death man wakes to the consciousness of his spiritual body, and of the objective and substantial reality of the spiritual world. According to the law of Discrete Degrees, the higher may enter into the lower, but not the lower into the higher. On the plane of physics, the ether may permeate the air; but not the air the ether. As matter can accordingly have no place in the spiritual world, there is no resurrection of the material body. "It is sown a natural, it is raised a spiritual body."

Every man undergoes his own judgment in the great meeting-place of all departed spirits, the intermediate "World of Spirits." This is effected by the unveiling, in the light of eternal realities, of his own essential character, "his ruling love," and led by this the spirit now seeks his own place, whether among the blessed or the lost. But there also occur, in the World of Spirits, at the end of each age or epoch of the world's history, a great general or Last Judgment, in which the spiritual throngs there are restored to their social order. This order becomes disturbed in the course of a long,  period by the accumulated confusion of incongruous and undeveloped states, and these intermediate spheres through which the heavenly influences descend to man need to be clarified of the invading clouds of evil. Through the clarifying and rectifying adjustments of such a judgment a new heaven and a new earth come into being. These great spiritual *Auf-klarungen* result in great moral and social revolutions below. The history of the world, therefore, has its counterpart and its true key in the history of these great general judgments in the World of Spirits ; and these are symbolically revealed in the Holy Scriptures in the great crises and epochal upheavals there described.

Swedenborg accordingly divides the history of the world into five ages or churches, each of which is characterized by "its understanding of the Word," i.e. by its mode of receiving and obeying revealed divine truth. Thus the real springs of the history of mankind are religious. These five spiritual ages of the world are, in their order:

I. The Adamic, or Eden Age: when the Divine was revealed intuitively to the child-like perception of the race, and "heaven lay about us in our infancy."

II. The Noahtic Age: the age of the living symbol, when symbols were chosen out of nature to stand for their correspondent spiritual essences or qualities. Here is the origin of hieroglyphics, of mythology, and of all spoken and written language.

III. The age of the dead symbol, when the living idea was lost and the natural object substituted in its place. This is the age of "Animism," the beginning of the historic ages and generally but erroneously accounted the beginning of religion. In reality the Animistic Age is that of religion's lowest decline from the primitive monotheism and child-like innocence of the Golden Age. This third, or first historic age, is that of the Israelitish Church, its written Word, its sacrificial worship and obligatory ritual. Revelation, which in the first age was by immediate vision, and in the second by symbol or allegory in which the heavenly realities were clothed, now finds in a fixed, divinely sanctioned ritual the only means of preserving the human race from the universal tendency to idol-worship and utter materialism.

IV. The Fourth Age is that of the Incarnation of the Word, which was necessitated when the letter of Holy Scripture was becoming of no effect through man's traditions, and when the salvation of mankind could be effected no longer by the presence of the Divine in nature, in symbol, in written law, or in the holy ritual now become dead. Only by the presence on earth of God incarnate in human nature, and His entering through human temptations into conflict with the hells, and by His victory over them, could the human race now be saved from self-destruction. The Christian Church thus founded is a dispensation of the letter of the Gospel; its end is prophesied by Christ Himself under the figure of the "end of the world," when the "love of many shall wax cold" and "the powers of the heavens shall be shaken." These prophecies are realized in the breaking up of the old conceptions of Christian truth based upon the "letter that killeth." The Christian Church, or the Fourth Spiritual Age, has in its turn, according to the divine prophecy, declined into tritheistic conceptions of God, the substitution of "faith alone" for charity, and the building up of purely material ideas of heaven and of the Lord's coming. But according to Christ's promise, the "parables" and "proverbs" of His own teaching are to give place to the "plain showing of the Father." This full and final revelation is, says Swedenborg, the opening of the spiritual sense of the Word, and is correspondingly prefigured in the language of Scripture as the coming of Christ "in the clouds of heaven, with power and great glory." The fuller revelation or coming of the Word no longer in the cloud, or symbol of the letter alone, but in the glory of spirit, produced in the spiritual world the great changes known as the Last Judgment. Hence the illusions of the old fictitious heavens pass away, and from the light of the new heavens, the Holy City, the Church in her final and perfected glory, descends to earth.

V. This is the inauguration of the Fifth Age of the World, the New Jerusalem "descending from God out of heaven," and whose religion shall be the worship of Jesus Christ in His Divine Humanity as God and the restored union of charity and faith in man's religious life. From this real inaugurative judgment, of which Swedenborg claims to have been a witness in the World of Spirits, have flowed down into this world of effects those marvelous changes which have constituted what all men testify to witnessing in these days the beginning of a new age of the world. It is a new spiritual age, distinguished by its mark as a "new church," in the broad and catholic sense in which Swedenborg uses this term.

# CHAPTER VII: THE DIVINE ALTRUISM, OR LOVE THE FINAL CAUSE OF CREATION

Swedenborg's entire system, regarded as a unit, finds its highest and most complete summarization in the doctrine of the Divine Love as the final cause of creation. In the earlier period the Infinite is regarded as the source of the universe, and creation begins with a conatus of motion in the Infinite. In the Principia we are told that all existence originates in motion from the Infinite; and with motion all modification, all variety, all force, all activity. Motion is subject to the threefold analysis, conatus, motion and force. Pure motion consists in the internal state, or conatus. It is differentiated from substance itself, and, while defined as the origin of all existence, still is declared to "originate in a more subtle element than that in which its activity is manifest." (Principia, i. 137). Again, we are told that motion itself is not substantial, but produces an appearance of substance and form. The internal motion is the only producing power, for without it there can be neither center nor circumference, neither contingency nor limit; but as a center and a conatus it can exist among finites and in space.

This concept of motion as the beginning of creation, mathematically or formally complete, lacks the element of substance itself, or the what that moves and is moved. It is only in the Sapientia Angelica that Swedenborg reaches the solution in the doctrine of the Good as the substance of all things and Truth as the Form of Good. This dual classification into Good and Truth as essential Substance and Form exhausts the entire realm of Being, and gives us the dynamic explanation of the universe. For in Good we have the end, the *Causa finalis* itself of creation, or that which is loved by the infinite Creator; and Truth is that inmost law, or Causa, efficient, by which all things take form in finite existence; and in use, or action, we have the end ultimated. Love, Wisdom and Use become now the divinely

humanized Infinite in place of the purely mathematical
conception of a causeless conatus and motion.

The Conatus now becomes that of the essential nature of
love itself. The essence of love is conjunction; its activity is only
reciprocal. There can be no love without an object, therefore
love, of necessity, creates an object, and from necessity makes
that object capable of freely reciprocating and returning the love
bestowed. Hence Swedenborg lays down the fundamental law
and cause of creation: "That the divine love and the divine
wisdom cannot be and exist except in other beings or existences
created from itself. For love consists in our willing what is our
own to be another's and feeling his delight as delight in
ourselves. It is an essential of love not to love itself, but to love
others and to to joined to them by love; it is also an essential of
love to be beloved by others, for thereby there is a conjunction...
Hence it is evident that the Divine love cannot be and exist
otherwise than in other beings or existences whom it loves and
by whom it is beloved; for when such a quality exists in all love
it must needs exist in the greatest degree, that is, infinitely in
Love Itself." (*Divine Love and Wisdom*, 47-8).

The reciprocal love which love demands from its object
can only be exercised by an object that is free. The universe as
an automaton acting only under the compulsion of divine law
would never furnish the response which the divine creative love
demands. Hence in all creation there is, with the evolution of
forms recipient of divine life, at the same time an evolution of
freedom. All created forms, even of the lowest mineral or
atmospheric atom, act from a certain conatus, or motive, as if
from some power of their own; but really as impelled by the
divine wisdom. The vegetative and the animal souls are but an
instinctive following of the laws of their special service in the
kingdom of uses. Only in man is reached the entire moral
freedom that is capable of returning a free answer to the love of
the Creator, and this implies equally the ability to turn away

from that love. Nature is but a ladder of uses by which all things ascend in higher and higher degrees of love and adoration to the Deity.

The highest exercise of freedom is in man's self-compulsion. The ability to compel one's self is the highest gift of God to man and is that upon which rests the whole order of creation, which is that of action and reaction. In order that there shall be an other to the Infinite and the Self-existent, that other must be finite and dead. Hence creation is a receding of the spheres of life emanating from God into those extremes where existence becomes utterly passive, inert and resistant; and the material world is that sphere of existence which has the ability to react against the living force of mind and life, and assert itself as the supreme and utter other to life and the infinite. Morally, freedom must consist in the ability to love self alone utterly and to deny truth; to turn light into darkness and heat into cold. All this is necessary to the creation of a moral world. But even in the dead object there must be a force and will to react, and this is divinely imparted and constitutes the gift of moral freedom, or the ability to act, according to Swedenborg's formula, *sicut a se* as if of oneself.

The principles of human freedom are thus set forth by Swedenborg in treating of the Laws of Divine Providence in his work entitled *The Apocalypse Explained* (1150).

"The fourth law of the Divine Providence is, That the understanding and the will should not be in the least degree compelled by another, since all compulsion by another takes away freedom; but that man should compel himself; for to compel himself is to act from freedom. Man's freedom belongs to his will; from the will it exists in the thought of the understanding; and by means of the thought it shows itself in speech and in the action of the body. For man says, when he wills anything from freedom, 'I will to think this,' 'I will to speak this,' and 'I will to do this.' From freedom of will he has also the faculty of thinking, of speaking and of acting, for the will gives this faculty because it is freedom. Since freedom belongs to man's will, it belongs also to his love, since nothing else in man constitutes freedom, but the love which belongs to his will."

"The reason is, that love is the life of man; for man is of the same quality as his love; consequently that which proceeds from the love of his will, proceeds from his life. Hence it is evident that freedom belongs to man's will, to his love and to his life; consequently, that it makes one with his *proprium* (or selfhood), and with his nature and disposition. Now because the Lord desires that everything which proceeds from Himself to man should be appropriated to man as if it were his own, for otherwise there would be in man no means of reciprocity by which conjunction is effected, therefore it is a law of the Divine Providence, that the understanding and the will of man should not be at all compelled by another."

The reconciliation of human freedom with divine sovereignty lies in the hidden, unconscious operation of the divine love upon the inmost affections of man.

"The reason that man does not perceive the operation of the Divine Providence is, that such perception would take away his freedom, and hence the faculty of thinking as if from himself, and with it also all the enjoyment of life, so that he would be like an automaton in which there is no principle of reciprocity. He would also be a slave, not a free man.

The principal cause that the Divine Providence moves so secretly that there is scarcely any vestige of it apparent, although it operates upon the most minute things of man's thought and will which regard his internal state, is, that the Lord continually desires to impress His love upon man, and through it His wisdom, and thus to create him into His image. Therefore it is that the operation of the Lord is upon man's love, and from it upon his understanding, and not from his understanding upon his love. The love, with its affections, which are manifold and innumerable, is not perceived by man except from a most general feeling, and that in so small a degree that it is scarcely perceptible at all; and yet man is to be led from one affection of love into another, according to the connection in which they are arranged, in order that he may be reformed and saved. This is incomprehensible, not only to man but also to the angels. If man discovered anything of these arcana, he could not be withdrawn from leading himself, even though it were continually from heaven into hell; notwithstanding he is constantly led by the Lord from hell into heaven; for from himself he constantly acts against (Divine) order, but the Lord constantly according to it." (*The Apocalypse Explained*, 1153).

The two forces of the creative love, therefore, lie at the base of human history; the wandering from God, the return to God; the descent or fall of man from the pristine innocence of his infantile or golden age down to the beginning of the Ascent in Christ, the New Adam, as humanity redeemed. The same law operates in the physical universe in two forces, the centrifugal force creating the "other" to the utmost extreme, the centripetal drawing the "other" back to itself. The equilibrium of the two forces establishing the fixed orbit of the planet is nature's reflection of the plane of human moral freedom. The creation of the other than itself by emanations is effected by degrees, or in successive atmospheres or auras, receding farther and farther from the source of life and motion until they become inactive or dead. In the Principia and the Regnum Animale these are treated of as physical spheres, even to the highest or universal aura in which the soul lives, as it were, in its own element, and which is above time and space and knows only the force of gravity or the attraction and repulsion which are most nearly allied to the forces of love and so of the moral world. Beneath these are successively the solar vortex, or the magnetic aura, the interplanetary aura, or the ether, and last of all the atmospheric air encompassing each planet. But in the Sapientia Angelica there is a wonderful transformation of these physical auras into the great dual correspondent system of the Two Worlds. Here the highest or innermost aura, the soul's atmosphere of the Regnum Animale, becomes the complete spiritual world, possessing its own sun and its own trinal succession of atmospheres or heavens, which at once are the types and furnish the emanating forces of the natural sun and of the physical atmospheres of the material world.

"When I was in enlightenment," says Swedenborg, meaning after his spiritual illumination, "I perceived that, from the light and the heat of the sun of the spiritual world, spiritual atmospheres were created one from another which were in themselves substantial; but... the sun from which all natural things proceed was created at the same time; and through this, in like manner by means of heat and light, three atmospheres environing the three former ones." (*True Christian Religion*, 76). Here we have the ultimate explanation of Swedenborg's doctrine of the Universe as an "animated mechanism." The material world, dead, inert, powerless of itself, as the "other" to the World of Spirits, is nevertheless actuated everywhere, even to its most minute atmospheric particles, by the corresponding particles of the spiritual atmospheres emanating from the sun of the spiritual world; which sun itself is the first effulgence of the Love and Wisdom of the Creator. The nature of the correspondence of the Two Worlds is thus set forth:

"The Divine Proceeding is what, around Him, appears to the angels as a sun; from this proceeds His Divine through spiritual atmospheres which He has created for the transmission of light and heat down to the angels, and which He has accommodated to the life both of their minds and their bodies, in order that they may receive intelligence from the light, also in order that they may see, and also that they may breathe according to correspondence; for the angels breathe like men. Also that they may receive love from the heat, may feel, and also in order that their hearts may beat according to correspondence; for the angels have a beating of the heart like men. These spiritual atmospheres are increased in density by discrete degrees… down to the angels of the lowest heaven, to whom they thus become accommodated. Hence it is that the angels of the highest heaven live as it were in a pure aura, the angels of the middle heaven as it were in ether, and the angels of the lowest heaven as it were in air. Under these atmospheres, in each heaven are earths on which the angels dwell." (*Divine Wisdom*, xii. 5).

"But it is to be known that the atmospheres originating from the sun of heaven, properly speaking, are not three, but six; three above the sun of our world and three below the sun of our world. The three above the sun of our world continually and immediately follow the three natural atmospheres, and cause man in the natural world to be able to think and feel. For the atmospheres originating from the sun of our world have not life in themselves, because they originate from a sun which is pure fire; whereas the atmospheres originating from the sun of heaven, which is the Lord, (Swedenborg is only intensifying the symbol when he says here that the sun of heaven is the Lord; for in *Divine Love and Wisdom*, 93, he declares that 'that sun is not God, but it is the proceeding from the Divine Love and the Divine Wisdom of God-Man; in like manner the light and heat from that sun... Beware of thinking that the sun of the spiritual world is God Himself- God is Man. The first proceeding from His love and wisdom is a fiery spiritual principle which appears in the sight of the angels as a sun.') have life in themselves because they originate from a sun which is pure love and pure wisdom. The atmospheres originating from the sun of our world, which is pure fire, cause those things which are in the earth and in the human body to remain in existence, and to be held together in connection, and not to be changed except according to the laws of natural order. Hence is the difference of things in the natural and spiritual worlds." (*Last Judgment*, 31).

Together with the translation of the divine love and wisdom as spiritual forms into their equivalents in the natural world's heat and light, there comes the representation of mental states in the spiritual world by the fixed times and spaces of the world of nature. (An interesting inquiry is prompted here as to the real relation of Swedenborg's doctrines of times and spaces being fixed in the natural world but existing as appearances, or phenomenally, in the spiritual world, with Kant's Phenomenology of the Spirit and the mediatory function in the Aesthetic of the time-and-space forms of judgment. The sources of this comparison are given in the Introduction on *Kant and Swedenborg* by Frank Sewall to Goerwitz's translation of Kant's Dreams of a Spirit Seer, published by Swan Sonnenschein & Co., London, 1900. It is an interesting coincidence that Swedenborg's little work on the Two Worlds, *De Commercio*, or *Influx*, published in 1769, should have been followed the next year by Immanuel Kant's Inaugural Address on the same theme, ' 'De Mundo sensibile et de Mundo intelligibile.') Times and spaces are determined in the spiritual world, says Swedenborg, by mental states of affection and thought; whereas they are determined in the natural world by the fixed standards of the earth's revolutions and dimensions. "While the spiritual times and spaces are, therefore, 'appearances' in the spiritual world, they are nevertheless real because they are necessary to the spirit's existence in an objective world, i.e. in a world of that which is other than himself; and such a world is morally necessary to man's exercise of the neighborly love which is the divine altruism or charity taking finite form in himself.

Heaven is therefore not a world of personalities submerged and dissolved in the one abyss of Being, but a world of the utmost distinctness of personality, each member being a distinct, special "form of charity" inspired with the love of others, and governed by the moral law of use, or of service to the neighbor, which is the fundamental law of creation from first to last and from last to first. The spatial distinctions of the spiritual world are, therefore, most real, because they are fundamental to the existence of man in neighborly relations; they are made even more real, by deriving their essence from living states of mind, than are the actual spaces and times of nature which depend on the mechanical standards of the  natural world.

## THE GREAT CATEGORIES: THE TWO KINGDOMS, THE THREE DEGREES

Finally, the great categories under which Swedenborg embraces all philosophical concepts are those of the Two Kingdoms Substance and Form, and of the Three Degrees End, Cause and Effect. The substance of things is their good; the form of things is their truth, or that by which the good appears and acts. But good, being also the end desired of the purpose in anything, is of the will and love; in like manner the form of its expression and activities is of the intellect. Hence all that pertains to substance is of the will or voluntary kingdom, as all that pertains to form is of the intellectual kingdom.

Man and nature not living of themselves, but as recipients of life from God, are constituted the twofold receptacles of the inflowing Divine. Man by his will and intellect receives the love and truth which are the essentials of his life; and nature receives the same inflowing principles in the heat and light and the respective physical forms and forces proceeding from the natural sun. So do the two worlds correspond in every minutest form and activity; and there is no form or function in one that may not be expressed in the terms of the other, the heat principle having everywhere a hidden relation to love and to good, the light principle being always manifestly related to truth. Upon this law of the basic or constructive relations of nature and spirit rests Swedenborg's doctrine of the internal sense of the divinely dictated Word, and of the possibility of its discovery by means of the Science of Correspondences. Upon the same dual constitution of nature rests all the imagery of language, the possibility of speech, and the laws of the mind's growth and education.

Besides the Two Kingdoms of Good and Truth as the essential substance and form of things, Swedenborg also furnishes philosophy with a new schema, of the activities of these two Kingdoms, in their respective three Discrete Degrees of End, Cause and Effect. These in their descending order he names the Celestial, the Spiritual and the Natural degrees of life. The celestial, characterized by love, is the highest of these planes of life in man or angel; the spiritual, where truth is the prevailing motive, is the mediate, and beneath these two there is the plane of action into which both descend and find their ultimate expression and use. To man's will and intellect there is added therefore the body of sense and action. The normal activity of the body is that of obedience to the intellect which carries out the desire of the will. So on the largest scale nature, as effect, is the body obedient to the impulses of spirit, or mind: and these are the great instrumental cause itself moved and actuated by the Supreme End, the Good of the divine love. God, Spirit, Nature; Love, Wisdom and Use such is the eternal Trinity which is reflected alike in the macrocosm and in the microcosm, in the universe and in man. By these successive degrees in their descending order God enters immediately into man from within and from above, without his knowledge, but as the very life itself from which man acts in all his conscious life. This is the subconscious, or instinctive life of the man. From below or from without, through the senses and into the plane of the body's activity and bondage to nature, God also enters into man's consciousness by the mediate influx of what the senses perceive and what the spirit imbibes from the world.

Intermediate between these inflowings is the rational

plane of the intellect and of the will's moral freedom, and here is born the spiritual man, or that principle where man leaves the animal and natural plane and enters the truly human plane of his immortal and angelic life. Here, as man consciously and of his free-will puts on the hitherto subconscious states of the higher life and makes them his own, he is born again as the child of God and made an heir to the kingdom of heaven. The ascending ladder of life now enables man to bring all the treasures of nature into the service of the Creator, and so to realize the reciprocal conjunction of God with the world. The spirit, when freed from the bonds of a time-and-space world and of a perishable body, finds its full social development in the *Maximus Homo*, or heaven, as the perfected society, the city of God. In heaven's life of mutual love and service, inspired by the devout adoration of the Creator, the divine altruism finds its complete actualization and Love, as the final Cause of creation, has attained its End.

## CHAPTER VIII: THE LAST DAYS AND DYING TESTIMONY

Swedenborg completed the True Christian Religion, that great summary of the Theology of the New Church, in his eighty-third year. After his repeated journeys abroad, chiefly to Holland and England, for the publishing of his works in those countries, where greater religious freedom prevailed than in his own, he sought in London the peaceful refuge of his last days. Here he lived in the simplest manner, beloved by little children and by the humble people with whom he lodged. Says Pastor Ferelius, the Chaplain of the Swedish Embassy, who was with him frequently during these last days:

"Some might think that Assessor Swedenborg was eccentric and whimsical, but the very reverse was the case. He was very pleasant and easy in company, talked on every subject that came up, accommodating himself to the ideas of the company, and he never spoke of his own views unless he was asked about them. But if he noticed that any one asked him impertinent questions, intending to make sport of him, he immediately gave such an answer that the questioner was silenced without being the wiser for his asking."

The dress that he usually wore when he went out to visit was a suit of black velvet made after an old fashion, with full ruffles at the wrist, a curious hilted sword, and a gold-headed cane. But he lived mostly a retired life. Mrs. Shearsmith, at whose house he lived, said that "he was a good-natured man; and that he was a blessing to the house; for that they had harmony and good business while he was with them." She also related that he announced before his death when this would take place, and "he was as much pleased as if he were to have a holiday or to go to some merrymaking."

Shortly before his death he wrote to Mr. Wesley that in the world of spirits he had learned of his desire to see him. Mr. Wesley on receiving this letter acknowledged to those present that this was indeed the case, although he had expressed this desire to no one, and he replied, fixing a time for a visit to Swedenborg when he should return to London from a six week preaching tour upon which he was about to set out. Swedenborg wrote in reply that it would then be too late, as he should "finally" enter the spiritual world on the twenty-ninth day of March. As the day of his death, thus foretold by himself, approached he was visited by the Pastor Ferelius for the purpose of administering to him the Sacrament of the Lord's Supper. On being exhorted by the clergyman in that solemn moment to declare whether he had written truly concerning his intromission into the spiritual world and what he had witnessed there, Swedenborg answered that every statement he had made concerning the opening of his spiritual sight and the things of the other life was true, and that he "could have written more if he had been permitted." When asked if he would receive the Sacrament he answered, "With thankfulness."

"I then asked," continued the clergyman, "whether he acknowledged himself to be a sinner." "Certainly, as long as I carry about me this sinful body," was the reply. And then, with much devotion, folding his hands and uncovering his head, he read the confession of sins and received the holy Sacrament. It was on his death-bed that he made the reply to the Rev. Thomas Hartley, who had asked him whether all that he had written was true, or whether any part or parts were to be excepted, "I have written nothing but the truth, as you will have more and more confirmed to you all the days of your life, provided you keep close to the Lord, and faithfully serve Him by shunning evils as sins against Him, and diligently searching His Word, which from beginning to end bears incontestable witness to the truth of the doctrines I have delivered to the world."

# SWEDENBORG

Swedenborg passed away in London on Sunday, March 29, 1772, aged eighty-four years. His remains were interred, with all the ceremonies of the Lutheran ritual, in the Swedish Ulrica Eleanora Church, Ratcliffe Highway, London, E., where their resting-place was marked later by a suitable memorial slab and tablet. In the Swedish House of Nobles, on October 7, a eulogy was pronounced upon him by M. Sandel, counselor of the Board of Mines, in the name of the Royal Academy of Stockholm. The Prime Minister, von Hopken, writing the following year to General Tuxen, remarks:

"The late Swedenborg was certainly a pattern of sincerity, virtue, and piety, and at the same time, in my opinion, the most learned man in this kingdom." (*Documents*, vol. ii. p. 410.)

Shortly before Swedenborg's death Dr. Messiter wrote to the Professor of Divinity at Edinburgh University: "As I have had the honor of being frequently admitted to the author's company when he was in London and to converse with him on various points of learning, I will venture to affirm that there are no parts of mathematical, philosophical, or medical knowledge, nay, I believe I might justly say, of human literature, to which he is in the least a stranger; yet so totally insensible is he of his own merit that I am confident he does not know that he has any; and, as he himself says of the angels, he always turns his head away at any encomium." And the same writer, addressing the Professor of Divinity at Glasgow, says of Swedenborg:

"I can with truth assert that he is truly amiable in his morals, most learned and humble in his discourse, and superlatively affable, humane and courteous in his behavior; and this joined with a solidity of understanding and penetration far above the level of an ordinary genius." (*Documents*, vol. ii. pp. 522, 525.)

# SWEDENBORG

Eighty years after Swedenborg's death a silver medal was struck in his honor by the Royal Swedish Academy. His remains still lay in the Swedish Church in London. His scientific and theological works were translated into English; the latter chiefly by the Swedenborg Society, established in London in 1810, and the former, including the *Principia*, the *Animal Kingdom, the Economy of the Animal Kingdom* and the *Chemistry*, by the labors of Charles Edward Strutt, of the Royal College of Surgeons in Edinburgh, the Rev. Augustus Clissold, M.A., of Exeter College, Oxford, and Dr. James John Garth Wilkinson, of the Royal College of Surgeons. Through the Swedenborg Society of London the theological works have also been translated and widely disseminated in various modern languages. The scientific and philosophical were, however, but partially published in the original Latin texts, and the English translations brought out in the middle of the last century have practically gone out of print. About the beginning of the present century a movement was made by the Swedenborg Scientific Association of America to publish the English editions of the Scientific "Works and to procure the publication and translation of the still unpublished MSS. preserved in the library of the Royal Academy of Sciences at Stockholm.

In the year 1903 the Royal Swedish Academy of Sciences at Stockholm, having been requested, through the Swedish legation at Vienna, to furnish certain information regarding Swedenborg's unpublished MS. De Cerebro, began an investigation of the Swedenborg MSS., which resulted in the appointment by the Academy of a Committee to edit and publish the entire series of the Scientific and Philosophical works in the original languages. Latin and Swedish. The Committee consisted of the following eminent scholars: Professor Gustaf Retzius, Alfred GK Nathorst, Svante Arrhenius, S. E. Henschen and Christian Loven. The volumes are being issued with special introductions in English by the respective editors, the general preface being furnished by Professor Retzius, the Chairman of the Committee; the literary editorship is in the hands of Mr. Alfred H. Stroh. The initial volume of this stately and monumental edition appeared in the year 1907. (Emanuel Swedenborg, *Opera Quaedam aut Inedita aut Obsoleta de Rebus Naturalibus nunc Edita sub Auspiciis Regiae Acadimiae Scientarum Sueciae: I Geologica et Epistolae* Prefatus est Gustav Retzius; Introductionem adjunxit, Alfred G. Nathorst; Editit Alfred H. Stroh, Holmiae; Ex Officin Aftonbladet. 1907, 4to. p. 344)

Since then the *Cosmologica*, with an Introduction by Svante Arrhenius, has been added. The introductions show that these volumes are given to the public, not as works of mere historic interest, but as containing facts and principles of the highest practical value to the science of this age principles which were too far in advance of the information of Swedenborg's own time to be then appreciated, but which are now being confirmed by constantly accumulating data, and are affording, by their unique and profound method, a guide of the greatest value for the progress of science in the future. Meanwhile the theological works of Swedenborg have been translated and published in more or less complete editions in many languages, including, besides the languages of Europe, Japanese and Hindi; and they are read by scholars and clergy of all denominations, Greek, Catholic and Protestant.

In the year 1908, at the request of the King of Sweden, moved by the desire of the Royal Swedish Academy of Sciences, the British Government consented to the removal of Swedenborg's remains to their native soil, after their repose in exile for one hundred and thirty six years. With impressive ceremonies they were taken from their long resting-place in the little Swedish Chapel in the Minories, in the presence of the representatives of the two governments and of the Lutheran Church and the Church of the New Jerusalem. The remains were conveyed to Sweden in a Swedish warship, and, after a suitable public reception, they were deposited in the Cathedral at Upsala, where by vote of the Swedish Parliament a monument is now in process of erection in the Bjelke chapel, immediately across the nave from that containing the monument to Linnaeus.

## CHAPTER IX: RELATIONS TO MODERN THOUGHT

*(At the desire of the publisher and with the consent of the author this chapter has been added, being furnished by the Rev. Isaiah Tansley, B.A., with a view to showing the present status and influence of Swedenborg's system in relation to modern thought and faith.)*

All great systems of philosophy and religion have had more or less influence on the contemporaries of their founders and on the opinion of succeeding generations. Socrates, although he did not found a school of thought, yet, by his conversation with his disciples and the Athenian youth, gave a trend to that spirit of inquiry which Plato, his disciple, followed in his works. Aristotle, the father of formal logic, worked out a philosophy which subsequently dominated scholasticism, and played an important part in medieval schools of philosophy. In more recent times Kant fundamentally influenced metaphysical thinking, on the question of space-and-time relations; while Berkeley practically founded a school of Idealism. It is not, therefore, remarkable that so original a thinker as Swedenborg should have attracted the attention of a certain class of minds. As shown in the preceding pages, he was a pioneer in the region of metaphysical and scientific speculation. Like Newton, he had a love for framing hypotheses; and, although he was attracted to the study of the ancient philosophers, particularly Aristotle, and, later, Christian Wolff, yet in a masterful way he cut out a path for himself. He, however, founded no school, and in his own country his works attracted only a minor attention. It was reserved for a few students in this country to recognize his great claims, and to translate some of his earlier writings from the Latin; and the remarkable revival of interest in his scientific works at the present moment indicates that what he wrote in his scientific period is of commanding interest. It is yet too soon, however, to say what the results of this renaissance may be, but it is certain that Swedenborg was far ahead of his day, both in scientific imagination and reach of ideas.

But, like Newton, Swedenborg gave his mind at a later period to the study of the Bible and questions arising out of it; unlike Newton's Biblical speculations, however, the works which Swedenborg wrote attracted thoughtful and scholarly minds almost from the first moment of their publication. So distinctive are the principles enunciated in his theological works that they were bound inevitably to give rise to a separate cult, or church. This is generally known as the New Church, popularly termed "Swedenborgianism," although this term was distinctly repudiated by Swedenborg. Early students in this country, becoming deeply impressed with the marked cleavage between the theology of Swedenborg and orthodoxy, felt compelled to dissociate themselves from current contemporary opinion, the result being the formation of societies for worship, as has been the case with other schools of religious thought.

Not being a philosophy merely, but a distinctive theology, a separate cult was a natural consequence. In a short time the societies of students and worshipers became an organization whose object was both ethical and propagandist. In this there is a parallel with Wesleyanism, although this cult was not based on a new theology, but on an enthusiasm for the deepening of the religious spirit. The particular cult which we are dealing with originated in London with a few men somewhat more than a hundred and twenty years ago; it soon gained adherents throughout this country, the Continent and America, and today has votaries in every part of the world.

It is worthy of remark that the theological writings of Swedenborg, from the commencement, had an attraction for Anglican clergy, among whom may be mentioned the Rev. Thomas Hartley, of Winwick, and the Rev. John Clowes, of St. John's, Manchester, two of the earliest translators of his works.

# SWEDENBORG

Swedenborgianism, other than a formal worship and particular cult, has found students among distinguished men, of whom Flaxman, the sculptor, S. T. Coleridge the poet, Dr. Garth Wilkinson, Coventry Patmore, Robert Browning, and others may be named, while in America Emerson marked his admiration for Swedenborg as a philosopher by including him in his Representative Men. The cult was very early carried to America, where, ever since, it has attracted thoughtful and instructed minds. It would not be difficult to show in some detail the influence of the principles of Swedenborg upon the theology of the past and the present were this the place; but we may say generally that while, on the one hand, criticism and a wider outlook upon problems affecting human nature are acting destructively upon theological views, the trend of thought in a more rational direction is due, we believe, to the principles and teachings of Swedenborg finding their way among thoughtful people. These principles, in their issue are, on the one hand, destructive of old, irrational conceptions; and, on the other, eminently constructive in the sense that they give us a philosophical system of faith which appeals to reason and the feeling for the fitness and logic of things.

Swedenborgianism differs from orthodox Christianity on the fundamental ground of the nature of the Deity, as based on absolute unity of function. There can be no rational conception of Being apart from unity in this regard. The unity and solidarity of the universe follow from this, while the forces of nature are but the expression of this unity in its primal origin in the Deity. The Incarnation was a particular manifestation of Infinite Being on the plane of matter and the demonstration of the Divine as essentially personal. All the functions of Being are derivable from the latter fact that of unity and personality; and in Swedenborg's teaching it is the antithesis of that distribution of Divine functions over the mysterious tri-personality of Being characteristic of orthodoxy. The central feature of Swedenborg's teachings, therefore, on this point is the assertion of this unity of

# SWEDENBORG

Being and function in the glorified and Divine Humanity of Jesus Christ as God manifest; it is this that renders his philosophy unique in its starting point and claims.

Without discussing the bearing of this on the question of revelation and inspiration, we may remark that this principle imparts to his ethics a definite form in its reference to human relations. And here, again, Swedenborg is divided impassably from the accepted principles of Christianity on the question of salvation. Ethics, that is duty, with Swedenborg is altruism, and altruism in his system involves an ideally organic whole. The functions of the individual are inseparably involved in the collective functions of the race; and, as the whole is conditioned by the parts, an infinite diversity of uses distributed among the individuals of the State will result in an altruistic unity and in the reciprocal action of the unit on the whole, and the whole on the unit.

The love of the neighbor is the basis of Swedenborg's ethics, the term. "neighbor" being extended to cover all human relations, the individual, one's country, the world and the Church. While this in no way ignores inevitable race differences, it demands the recognition of the common heritage of the human family, and holds out the hope of an ultimate international unity and brotherhood. This is the end, purpose and climax of Swedenborg's ethical philosophy, and is the very outcome of his conception of Infinite Being as the Infinite Good, or the *summum bonum*. Whether in discussing the fundamental and complex problems involved in conceptions of Deity and immortality or the question of duty, the whole of Swedenborg's philosophy culminates, then, in this doctrine of Use, or Altruism, which will mean, in ultimate practice, a perfectly ordered world and the happiness of the race.

While Swedenborg's doctrine of Use, or Altruism, bears some resemblance to Plato's conception of the functions of the state and the individual, it is necessarily dissimilar because of their different point of view, and the mental atmosphere in which they lived. Swedenborg found his ideal State in the government and organic unity of the Divine Kingdom, in the heavens of which, as he declares, he had conscious knowledge during a long period of unique spiritual experiences. And in bringing the knowledge thus gained to bear on human problems, he sets forth the principles which must rule in the human organic world, showing that a true philosophical theology has a direct and intimate bearing on life, duty and practice, and not only in this world but the world to come. For on the question of the immortal life Swedenborg writes with reasoned and strong conviction, the outcome of his unique experiences. What, in the Christian view, is vague and nebulous he renders emphatically clear, not only by telling the result of his own observations in the other world, but in philosophic deduction from facts. In the light of his argument and statements man stands out clearly in the other life as a perfect, complete, conscious, rational being. This is the antithesis of the shadowy conceptions undeniably current among Christians today. It coordinates the mundane life with the spiritual, indicates the unity of mankind in both worlds, and imparts a true dignity and grandeur to the idea of immortality.

Man, then, is a spiritual being not only intrinsically as to personality, but also in his relation to God and the world. He is not an accident of evolution, but the ultimate factor of creation. The world, the non-ego, being the plane of man's existence, it is pervaded by that spirituality which renders it intelligible. In fact, for Swedenborg the whole universe is the expression of the spiritual. It exists from the Divine; God is in it by immanence and discreted from it by transcendence, and therefore infinite love and infinite intelligence are manifest in it and discernible in it; which, working in men according to the degree of each one's finite reception shall, in the fulfillment of the ultimate Divine purpose, realize a spiritual Kingdom wherein justice, peace, righteousness and brotherhood will be the permanent elements.

If this be a true presentation, in brief, of some of the chief points in Swedenborg's theological philosophy then it seems explicable why its range of influence is not inconsiderable, and why it has commended itself to men of a studious and practical turn of mind.

# SWEDENBORG

## APPENDIX

### BIOGRAPHIES

An exhaustive and trustworthy account of Swedenborg, his life, his work, and his relations with his contemporaries is to be found in the *Documents Concerning Swedenborg*, in three volumes, compiled and edited by R. L. Tafel, A.M., Ph.D., Swedenborg Society, 1 Bloomsbury Street. Excellent biographies are also: *Swedenborg and His Mission*, by Benjamin Worcester; *Emanuel Swedenborg: a Biography*, by J. J. Garth Wilkinson; Hobart's *Life of Swedenborg*; *Emanuel Swedenborg: A Lecture* by the Rev. John Hyde. Also Articles in *Prospective Review*, May 1850, *National Review*, 1858; *Herder on Swedenborg in Werke zur Philosophic der Geschichte*, vol. xii. pp. 110-25; Goerres, *Emanuel Swedenborg, Seine Visionen und sein Verhaltniss zur Kirche*, 1827; Doerner, *Geschichte Protestantischer Theologie* (Munich, 1867); *Sammlung von Urkunden*, Dr. J. F. Immanuel Tafel (Tubingen, 1841). Also the quite recent works: *Emanuel Swedenborg; his Life, Teaching and Influence*, by George Trobridge (Frederick Warne & Co., London and New York), pp. 140; *Swedenborg, af Ernst Liljedahl: De Storsta Markesmannen*, IX Stockholm (Hugo Gebers), p. 72; *Grunddragen af Swedenborgs Lif*, af Alfred H. Stroh (Stockholm: Nykyrkliga Bokforlaget, 1908, 811), p. 176; *A Great Thinker: Review of Swedenborg's Complete Works*. Rotch Edition, by Mayo Hazeltine (Reprint from the New York Sun), 1908; *Le Prophete du Nord: Vie et Doctrine de Swedenborg, avec portrait et diagrammes*, par Charles Byse (Paris: Librairie Fischbacher, 33, rue de la Seine).

## BIBLIOGRAPHY

*A Bibliography of Swedenborg*, Royal 4to. Compiled by the Rev. James Hyde: Swedenborg Society, London.

# SWEDENBORG

The works of Swedenborg have been translated for the larger part into English, German, French, Swedish, Danish and Italian. Single treatises have been published in Russian, Spanish, Norwegian, Dutch, Welsh, Icelandic, Japanese, Arabic, Hindi, and Esperanto. The Swedenborg Society, 1 Bloomsbury Street, London, publishes a uniform edition of the Theological Works in twenty-nine volumes, and the Scientific Works in ten volumes, several of the latter being out of print and new editions in preparation.

The American Swedenborg Printing and Publishing Society, 3 W. 29th Street, New York, publishes the Theological Works in a complete and uniform edition, and has in course of production a very elegant edition in Latin, and one in Latin and English. A considerable number of Swedenborg's works were published posthumously, including the extensive exposition the *Apocalypse Explained*. Thirteen folio volumes of photo-lithograph copies of the original MSS. in the Royal Library at Stockholm have been published through the donations of followers in England and America. The collateral literature connected with Swedenborg and the New Church is very extensive. The entries under "Swedberg Swedenborg" in the Catalog of the British Museum number between five and six hundred.

## PUBLISHED WORKS IN ENGLISH

### A. THEOLOGICAL

*The Apocalypse Explained according to the Spiritual Sense*. Six vols.

*The Apocalypse Revealed*, wherein are disclosed the Arcana there foretold which have hitherto remained concealed.

*Arcana Coelestia*. The Heavenly Arcana contained in the

Holy Scripture or Word of the Lord unfolded, beginning with the Book of Genesis i., together with wonderful things seen in the World of Spirits and in the Heaven of Angels. Twelve vols.

*The Athanasian Creed* and Subjects connected therewith.

*Brief Exposition of the Doctrine of the New Church.*

*Canons: or the Entire Theology of the New Church* (in outline). Posthumous.

*Delights of Wisdom pertaining to Conjugal Love.*

*The Coronis*, Appendix to the True Christian Religion. Treating of the Four Churches on the Earth from the Creation of the World, their Periods and their Consummation. Of the New Church which is to succeed those Four, which will be truly Christian and the Crown of the Preceding ones, etc.

*Angelic Wisdom concerning the Divine Love and the Divine Wisdom.*

*Angelic Wisdom concerning the Divine Providence.*

*Doctrine of Life for the New Jerusalem.* From the Commandments of the *Decalogue.*

*Doctrine of the New Jerusalem concerning Charity.*

*Doctrine of the New Jerusalem concerning Faith.*

*Doctrine of the New Jerusalem concerning the Lord.*

*Doctrine of the New Jerusalem concerning the Sacred Scripture.*

# SWEDENBORG

*The Earths in our Solar System*, which are called Planets, and the Earths in the Starry Heavens. With an Account of their Inhabitants and also of the Spirits and Angels there: from what has been seen and heard.

*Heaven and its Wonders and Hell*: from things heard and seen.

*The Intercourse of the Body and the Soul* (De Commercio).

*An Account of the Last Judgment and Babylon destroyed*, showing that all the predictions in the Apocalypse are at this day fulfilled.

*The New Jerusalem and its Heavenly Doctrine*, according to what has been heard from Heaven, to which is prefixed Information regarding the New Heaven and the New Earth.

*The Spiritual Diary of Emanuel Swedenborg*. Being the record during eighteen years of his supernatural experience. Five vols.

*Summary Exposition of the Internal Sense of the Prophets and Psalms*.

*The True Christian Religion*. Containing the Universal Theology of the New Church.

*The White Horse mentioned in the Apocalypse*.

## B. SCIENTIFIC AND PHILOSOPHICAL

*The Infinite, and the Final Cause of Creation*.

# SWEDENBORG

*Motion and Position of the Earth and the Planets.*

*Ontology,* or the Signification of Philosophical Terms.
Principia, or the First Principles of Natural Things: being New
Attempts towards a Philosophical Explanation of the Elementary
World. Translation from the Latin by the Rev. Augustus Clissold,
M.A. Two vols.

*Principles of Chemistry,* with other Treatises. Translated
by Strutt.

*The Economy of the Animal Kingdom*, considered
Anatomically, Physically and Philosophically. Two vols.
Translated by J. J. Garth Wilkinson.

*The Animal Kingdom.* Considered Anatomically,
Physically and Philosophically. Two vols. Translated by J. J.
Garth Wilkinson.

*Scientific and Philosophical Treatises*: on Anatomy,
Physiology, Psychology and Philosophy. Published by the
Swedenborg Scientific Association.

*The Soul; or, Rational Psychology.* Translated and
edited by Frank Sewall.

*Miscellaneous Observations* connected with the Physical
Sciences. Translated by Strutt.

*On Generation*. Posthumous. Translated by J. J. Garth
Wilkinson.

## C. COLLATERAL TREATISES

*Emanuel Swedenborg as an Anatomist and Physiologist.*
By Professor Dr. Gustaf Retzius. Published under the Auspices

of the Swedenborg Scientific Association: Bryn Athyn Pa. 1903.

*Emanuel Swedenborg sasom Hjarnanatom och Fysiologisk Psykology*: af Alfred H. Stroh, M.A. (Upsala. 1909.)

*The Cartesian Controversy at Upsala*, 1663-1689, and its connection with Swedenborg's Nebular Hypothesis. By Alfred H. Stroh. From the Proceedings of the Third International Congress for Philosophy (Heidelberg, 1908.)

*Swedenborg's Influence upon Goethe*. Address before the American Philosophical Association, 1905. In New Philosophy (Quarterly). 1906. By Frank Sewall.

Emanuel Swedenborg's *System der Naturphilosophie* besonders in seiner Beziehung zu Goethe Herderschen Anschauungen. Inaugural Dissertation by Dr. Hans Schlieper. (Berlin. 1901.)

*Swedenborg's Physiology of the Brain*. Address of Dr. Max Neuburger of the University of Vienna before the Convention of Naturalists and Physicists in Hamburg. Vienna Medical Weekly, 1901, No. 44.

*Kant and Swedenborg*. Introduction to Kant's Dreams of a Spirit Seer (translated by Emanuel Goerwitz), by Frank Sewall. (Swan Sonnenschein & Co., 1900.)

*Der Angebliche Mysticismus* Kants. Robert Hoar. (Brugg. 1895.)

*The New Metaphysics*: or, the Law of End, Cause and Effect. By Frank Sewall. (J. Speirs, London. 1887.)

*Swedenborg and Modern Idealism*: a Retrospect of Philosophy from Kant to the Present Time. By Frank Sewall. (J.

Speirs.)

*The New Philosophy.* A Quarterly Magazine devoted to the Interests of the Swedenborg Scientific Association. Lancaster, Pa., U.S.A.

**THE END**

9 7 9 8 6 4 7 6 4 5 0 2 9